EMBRACING THE UNCERTAIN

A Lenten Study for Unsteady Times

Also from Magrey R. deVega:

Embracing the Uncertain:
40 Devotions for Unsteady Times

Awaiting the Already:
An Advent Journey Through the Gospels

One Faithful Promise:
The Wesleyan Covenant for Renewal

Magrey R. deVega

EMBRACING THE UNCERTAIN

A *Lenten* Study for Unsteady Times

Abingdon Press / Nashville

EMBRACING THE UNCERTAIN
A Lenten Study for Unsteady Times

Copyright © 2017 Abingdon Press
All rights reserved.

This book is printed on elemental chlorine-free paper.

Library of Congress Cataloging-in-Publication Data has been requested.

ISBN 978-1-5018-40586

17 18 19 20 21 22 23 24 25 26 — 10 9 8 7 6 5 4 3 2 1
MANUFACTURED IN THE UNITED STATES OF AMERICA

To Karangalan Salamon, Hernan Andone, and
Zenaida Andone, for your faithful example of
steadfast love and constant prayer;

To Christopher, Jean, Doug, and Teresa, for helping
me embrace the uncertainties of my life;

To Dad, Mom, Genniser, Mykel, Amanda,
Sara, Kai, Maya, Noah, and Emma,
for keeping me steady during unsteady times;

And to Grace and Madelyn, for showing
me proof of the Resurrection every day.

CONTENTS

INTRODUCTION

Doesn't it feel like just yesterday that we celebrated Jesus' birth? Hasn't it felt like just a few weeks since we took down our Christmas trees and sent off our thank-you notes? People used to tell me all the time to enjoy my kids while they're young, because they grow up so fast. But in the church's liturgical calendar, no kid grows up faster than Jesus. In the weeks since Christmas Day, Jesus has aged thirty-three years!

If you stop and think about it, you'll find there are some interesting differences between the timing of Christmas and Lent every year.

Christmas Day is predictable. It is always on December 25. It is easy to order our lives and activities around it. It's never in November, never creeps into January. School semesters can schedule a break around it; retail establishments base their revenue projections on it. There is something constant and comforting about this fixed holiday.

But Lent and Ash Wednesday move around. Ash Wednesday occurs forty-six days before Easter Sunday, which is celebrated—are you ready for this—on the first Sunday after the first full moon that occurs on or following the spring equinox on March 21. This means that Ash Wednesday can occur as early as the first week in February or as late as the second week in March. That's a variation of nearly thirty-five days!

What that means is that Lent often sneaks up on us. It catches us off guard. It can disrupt our planning. Sometimes the school spring breaks are during Holy Week, and sometimes they're not. Sometimes the stores have time between their Valentine's Day hearts and their chocolate Easter eggs, and sometimes they don't.

It's a lot like life, when you think about it. We can know with certainty when we were born; we cannot say the same for when we will die. Likewise, Christmas is comforting in its constancy, but Lent is elusive and unpredictable.

Perhaps it is best that it be this way, for Advent and Lent portray two very different ways of following Jesus. The former calls us to the comforts of life and light; the latter calls us to reflect with humility and penitence. Most of us find it easier to celebrate the comfort and hope of Jesus' birth than to risk the way of the cross. We tend to gravitate toward the Advent mode of following Jesus:

- We easily and gladly claim love, joy, peace, and hope when times are going well. But we cannot predict with any certainty the timing or severity of the chaos that is sure to greet us down the road.
- We often celebrate the Advent of Christ in our lives, while ignoring our need to be crucified with him.
- We can believe with certainty the constant faithfulness and love God has given to us through Christ. But we are blind to the sin that festers and blooms within the subsoil of our existence.
- We can trust with absolute conviction what God has done for us through Christ. But we can be much more reluctant in determining what we can do for God in the name of Christ.
- We can live as secularized Christians, or what John Wesley would call "Almost Christians," in which celebration is a given but discipline is elusive. In that case, a life of mere good deeds and a life of sincere, righteous faith are worlds apart.

Lent is the sobriety before the celebration. On Ash Wednesday, the touch of ash on our skin and the reminder that we are dust call to mind the precariousness of our existence. Relationships break, discernment fails, confidence falters, fears loom, shame builds, temptations grow, doubt increases. Chaos convenes without notice, even in times of apparent blessing. Uncertainty abounds in our individual lives and in the twenty-first-century world in which we live. And lurking beneath all of it is one of the few guarantees in life: the reality of our own mortality.

Lent is an invitation for us to engage life's uncertainties, not ignore them.

Regardless of how subtly this Lenten season has snuck up on us, it always starts in the wake of Transfiguration Sunday. That story is the theological midway point in Matthew, Mark, and Luke, after which the Gospel writers prepare the reader for the journey to Jerusalem. (The equivalent moment in John, who does not write about the Transfiguration, is in chapter 7, in which Jesus travels and begins to teach in Jerusalem.)

After the Transfiguration, with every step from that moment on, we notice something about the ground beneath us. The closer we get to Jerusalem, and the closer we get to the cross, the more we realize that the sands are shifting below our feet. Everything we thought we could count on, every foundation we thought was firm enough to build our lives on, becomes something like tectonic plates that are not only moving, but quaking.

Just look at the post-Transfiguration, pre-Passion, wholly Lenten stories in the second half of these Gospels:

- Look at the desperate father who came to Jesus for more than the healing of his son. His words, "I have faith; help my lack of faith!" come from a man who is not sure how to have faith when his world and his mind are swimming with doubts (Mark 9:14-29).

- Look at Peter, who was pondering the frailty of human relationships and wrestling with how to forgive someone who had wronged him (Matthew 18:21-22).
- Look at the anonymous voice from the crowd, whose dispute with his brother over an inheritance prompted Jesus to teach them about how to find security in a future filled with worry (Luke 12:13-34).
- Look at Mary and Martha, grieving over the death of their brother Lazarus, angry at Jesus for his supposed indifference, and staring squarely at the reality of their finite human existence (John 11:1-44).
- Look at Zacchaeus, the tax collector who made a career out of cheating people, coming to the blessed realization that his corrupt ways did not constitute the most holy life (Luke 19:1-10).
- And look at Jesus, whose blood-stained prayer in the garden of Gethsemane was a struggle to discern the mystery and complexity of God's will (Matthew 26:36-46).

Each of these characters is a signpost in the Gospel narrative, pointing down at a world filled with uncertainty, but pointing us forward to a cross that can show us how to follow Jesus with courage, hope, and obedience.

It is only by embracing the uncertain that we can fully acknowledge the power and the proof of the Resurrection on Easter Sunday. It is at the empty tomb that we discover that the ground has settled, our footing is sure, and that there is only one source for a firm foundation upon which to build our lives.

May this forty-day journey be for you an invitation to look deeply within yourself, to determine what resides in the uncertain—in the shadowy, untenable, and unreliable parts of your soul. May you identify that within your life which must be acknowledged, confessed, and ultimately, through the glory of Easter, overcome by God's grace.

Ready or not, welcome to this Lenten journey.

ONE

THE DESPERATE FATHER AND THE UNCERTAINTY OF FAITH

Read Mark 9:14-29

It does not take long for the shimmer of the Transfiguration experience to fade as Jesus and the disciples briskly reenter the problems of the real world. No sooner had Jesus, James, John, and Peter come down from the mountain where the Transfiguration took place than they saw a large crowd gathered. Several religious officials were arguing with the other disciples.

In the center of the discussion was a man whose son was possessed by what the Bible says was an evil spirit. It is possible that it was a literal demon, or it could have been the biblical writers' best way to describe a dark emotional and mental state, rendering the boy uncontrollable and mute.

However, as much as the boy was suffering from debilitating physical elements, the real issue at stake was what was happening spiritually. The child's father had approached the disciples with a conviction and confidence that simply coming to them would guarantee his son's healing. But as often happens when one chooses to follow Jesus, the man did not get what he was hoping for. The ending did not meet his expectations. His boy was still as sick as ever, and he was starting to lose faith. The disciples were not able to deliver.

That's when Jesus showed up, and the man piped up. He shared with Jesus his son's whole medical case file: Foamy mouth. Grinding teeth. Stiff muscles (Mark 9:18).

In response to hearing the whole diagnosis and the disciples' inability to help, Jesus responds with what appears to be an odd rebuke: "You faithless generation, how long will I be with you? How long will I put up with you?" (Mark 9:19).

Apparently the father hadn't caught Jesus in the best of moods. But maybe what Jesus was offering here was not so much a rebuke of the man, but a reminder to everyone listening that there would be a time when he would not be with them. They would not have his real-life, flesh-and-blood presence to see, hear, touch, and experience. And if they were having trouble believing Jesus when he *was* around, imagine what it would be like when he wasn't.

Jesus asked the disciples to bring the boy to him, at which point the boy's symptoms were put on full display. He fell to the ground, rolled around, and foamed at the mouth. The father explained that his symptoms had been with him since childhood and that he'd had several near-death experiences. He was lucky to still be alive, but the condition of his life was really no way to live.

"If you can do anything, help us!" he cried to Jesus (Mark 9:22). Show us compassion. Please do something.

"If you can do anything?" Jesus asked, as if incredulous that the man would doubt his ability. Then he reminds the boy's father, "All things are possible for the one who has faith" (Mark 9:23).

Now pause for a moment and think about how this father's anguish resonates with your own spirit today. For then the father put it bluntly: "Immediately the father of the child cried out, 'I believe; help my unbelief!'" (Mark 9:24 NRSV).

What a peculiar response. In his distress, the father appeared to say two contradictory things at once. Belief *and* unbelief. Yes *and* no. I get it, but I don't get it. As you and I read the father's words, we wish we had the ability to ask him the obvious clarifying questions: "What did you mean by that, sir? How can you believe and not believe?" We don't understand, and we would really like some certainty.

How in the world do we make sense of this statement?

However

If a grammar teacher were there, she might give him some grammatical advice. "You seem to be missing a word in between those two statements, something to help us understand the relationship between 'I believe' and 'Help my unbelief.' What you need is a conjunction."

Looking at the original Greek doesn't offer any help. There is no conjunction there, so many English translations don't render one, either. Rather than having the luxury of asking this father personally for clarification, we are left to play fill-in-the-blank with the Gospel. There's a blank there, and it's asking for us to fill it.

First, we try the word *however*. That seems reasonable enough. "Lord, I believe. . . . However, . . ." That certainly seems to work because it is true for many of us. Yes, we believe. However, we still doubt. Yes, we live with certainty. However, we still have our jitters.

We spend so much of our formative years acquiring knowledge to dispel uncertainty. We learn mathematics and science to figure out how the world works. We develop skills in language and communication to acquire and share ideas with others. We educate ourselves in philosophy, history, and sociology to determine our place in the grand scheme of human civilization. And every time we learn something, we add it to an ever-widening foundation upon which we can frame our existence.

However, . . .

There are also those moments that challenge our most basic assumptions. As we moved from adolescence into adulthood, we were confronted by the unpredictability and chaos of life. Suffering and tragedy. Grief and loss. We experience events that shock us into the sobering reality that things don't always turn out the way we expect or the way we hope.

Like tectonic plates or frayed fabric, those basic assumptions we have made about the world shift beneath our feet, or get tugged and pulled within us. All the knowledge and certainty we've carefully built up suddenly come into question. Sometimes that happens in a college classroom, in which a free exchange of ideas poses a question you had never considered. Sometimes that happens in a church Bible study, when someone offers a different way to interpret a Scripture passage that challenges the way you approach the faith. Sometimes that happens at a graveside, or in a doctor's office, or in a courtroom, or anywhere else in which the realities of life grab a singular thread and pull on the tightly wound fabric of your beliefs and your assumptions.

Life can be like a constant pendulum swing between certainty and uncertainty. Between belief and unbelief. And it is rare that those two extremes conveniently coexist.

Lord, I believe. *However*, help my unbelief.

To put the word *however* in the man's sentence is to suggest that belief and unbelief, certainty and doubt, are an uneasy mix, even mutually exclusive. The word *however* says that we try as hard as we can to be confident, but acknowledge that we still fall short. Is that the nature of this father's peculiar response to Jesus? Is it equal parts profession and confession? An affirmation of his belief, yet a repentance for his own shortcomings?

Therefore

Well, if *however* is a reasonable possibility, I would like to suggest another, maybe one that is more likely, and even more suitable for your situation today.

How about the word *therefore*?

"I believe; *therefore*, help my unbelief."

Unlike *however*, the word *therefore* suggests that belief and unbelief go together. Because belief exists, unbelief exists as well. I believe;

therefore, help the unbelief that naturally comes with it. In other words, certainty and uncertainty are not mutually exclusive, but are necessary co-companions in your journey of life. They are the yin and the yang. They exist in our lives just as light creates shadows. If you have one, you must have the other. The more you grow in your understanding of who you are, the world around you, and the reality of God in your life, the more you must be aware of what you don't know and be ready for the surprises that lie ahead.

The presence of the word *therefore* would be a reminder to us that tension and ambiguity in life are not always bad things. Struggling with what we know and don't know does not convey how weak we are but simply how human we are. Faith is not the absence of doubt, but the embrace of it and ultimately the transformation of it. Likewise, courage is not the elimination of fear, but the regular interaction with it and conscious choice against it.

The truth of the matter is, we live in a time when there is more value in ambiguity and shades of gray than there is in rigid, dogmatic certainty. Our world will be made better not by the extremists on the fringes who think everyone else has it wrong, but by those in the center who believe there is value in dialogue. Uncertainty is a certain part of life, and with its embrace can come transformation.

It's interesting to note Jesus' response to the father who cried, "I believe; help my unbelief!" Whereas in other stories, Jesus praised people for their faith or indicated how impressed he was, Jesus said nothing to this man. Nothing at all.

Mark moves on with the story as if the man had not said a word. Because of this, we are led to believe that Jesus found the man's response to be neither troublesome nor noteworthy. Perhaps it is because he found it to be so natural. Whereas we might labor over what the man's true motivations were deep down, it seems that Jesus knew.

He knew that the man was simply exhibiting all that it meant to be human. This, after all, was the same Jesus who would say later in his life, in the same breath, "Take this cup of suffering away from me. However—not what I want but what you want" (Mark 14:36).

Jesus knew what it meant to be internally conflicted, so Jesus gave this man the most salvific non-response in the Gospels. Instead of responding verbally, Jesus moved on to the important business at hand. He entered right into the midst of the man's tension and spoke the demon out of his son's body:

> *Noticing that the crowd had surged together, Jesus spoke harshly to the unclean spirit, "Mute and deaf spirit, I command you to come out of him and never enter him again." After screaming and shaking the boy horribly, the spirit came out. The boy seemed to be dead; in fact, several people said that he had died. But Jesus took his hand, lifted him up, and he arose.*
>
> (Mark 9:25-27)

Jesus' response to the man's anguished, conflicted cry was to bring healing.

There is a lesson here for all of us. When we are at our most vulnerable, at the point of acknowledging our deepest tensions, we need neither be judged nor praised. We can simply be transformed. Healed. Brought to a maturity that neither ignores nor condemns uncertainty, but embraces it for its benefit.

If we insert the word *therefore* into the father's cry, then we receive this great lesson: don't settle for easy answers in life. Don't ever stop the thirst for learning, for checking your assumptions, for embracing the unknown. Don't ever stop maturing in your faith. Admit your doubts and acknowledge your questions.

And if you are looking for a model in recent Christian history of someone who was able to hold his belief and unbelief together in balance, consider Thomas Merton.

A Prayer by Thomas Merton

Thomas Merton was a Roman Catholic monk of the Trappist order who wrote over seventy books on the spiritual life. His autobiography

The Seven Storey Mountain was named one of the hundred most important books in the twentieth century by *National Review*. It details his remarkable conversion to Christianity, from his teen years as an agnostic to when he became one of the most significant Christian authors of our time.

One of his most famous prayers was part of his book *Thoughts in Solitude*, first published in 1956. It touches on a universal theme of longing in the midst of confusion, as well as a desire to do God's will even when discernment of it seems impossible. It conveys an intimacy with God when God seems most distant and at the same time a depth to the spiritual life when all one has is rote practice. It is the fusion of these extremes, in creative tension, that has contributed to the power of this prayer for many people.[1]

The prayer's powerful authenticity is evident from its first few lines: "My Lord God, I have no idea where I am going. I do not see the road ahead of me. I cannot know for certain where it will end."[2] These words are a remarkable amount of candor coming from one so hallowed as Merton, but it is that honesty that makes his witness so comforting and relatable to the rest of us. Like Mother Teresa's "Come Be My Light" or Dietrich Bonhoeffer's "Who Am I?" Merton's prayer gives us permission to reveal our innermost doubts.

Merton goes on to admit that he does not truly know himself, and that he may not in fact be following God's will even when he thinks he is. Merton doesn't claim a perfect understanding of the Christian faith; he doesn't even state that such knowledge is ultimately and fully possible. But he believes as he prays that his desire to do God's will is in itself pleasing to God. And it is a good thing that simply having that desire is enough, for sometimes that is all we are capable of offering. Just like the father of the demon-possessed boy, Merton lived with this odd and seemingly untenable juxtaposition between belief and unbelief. But such a moment of tension, while uncomfortable, is stasis nonetheless. And it can be a time of great strengthening for our spiritual commitments.

With all of the uncertainty embedded into his prayer, Merton claims one final, incontrovertible truth: we are not alone. God is always with us, even in moments when God seems absent or distant. God will never leave you to confront life's trials alone.

In the honest proclamation by the father in Mark's Gospel, which is echoed in Merton's prayer, we have been given rich resources to embrace the uncertainty in our lives. Commit yourself to following the will and way of Jesus, acknowledging that life may not always meet your expectations or understanding. Those moments of uncertainty need not dispel your belief, but may actually strengthen it. Your desire to please God may, in fact, be pleasing to God in itself.

Reflection Questions

1. Have you or a loved one ever experienced something akin to the dark emotional or mental state of the young boy in Mark 9:14-29? What kind of support and resources are helpful amid such a crisis?

2. When has doubt or suffering ever challenged your beliefs and assumptions about the Christian faith?

3. How did those doubts feel contradictory to your beliefs? In what ways might they even have eventually strengthened your convictions?

4. How would you describe the relationship between faith and certainty?

5. Read the first words of Thomas Merton's prayer again. What parts are helpful to you? Does the knowledge that even a formidable writer and teacher like Merton felt doubt bring comfort to you? How?

6. Where is there uncertainty in your life, especially in your faith? What would it mean to embrace that uncertainty? How might doing so lead you to deeper faith?

Embracing the Uncertain

Spend some time writing a prayer in your own words that expresses your doubts and your confidence in God. You might even journal the specific nature of your doubts that in some way connect to the concerns of the father in Mark 9 for his son. Write out all the ways in which you find yourself saying, "I believe; help my unbelief."

Prayer

God, thank you for grounding me with confidence and guiding me through doubt. I offer you my very best intentions to follow you, grateful for your grace and forgiveness when I falter and fall short. I believe; help my unbelief. Amen.

TWO

PETER AND THE UNCERTAINTY OF FORGIVENESS

Read Matthew 18:21-22

It should be no surprise that one of the marks of Christian character is the capacity to forgive. It is part of the prayer that Jesus taught us to pray: "Forgive us our trespasses, as we forgive those who trespass against us." He spent a significant portion of his greatest sermon, the Sermon on the Mount, talking about loving your enemies and turning the other cheek. And it was so important to Jesus that he spent some of his final, fleeting energy to forgive those who crucified him, praying, "Father, forgive them, for they don't know what they're doing" (Luke 23:34).

But when it all comes down to it, we can acknowledge how uncertain we feel about this whole subject of forgiveness. Why should we forgive? How can we forgive when it is so hard to do so? What difference does forgiveness make, anyway?

Apparently, we are not alone in our wondering. Peter was wrestling with this question as well. And if anything, Jesus' answer drew Peter into even more uncertainty about forgiveness.

You've got to love the way Jesus answered questions. Sometimes he would answer them directly. But often he wouldn't. Sometimes he would answer questions with other questions. Or with silence. Or by telling a story. And then there were times he avoided answering them altogether.

Jesus must have loved surprising his questioners with these indirect answers or non-answers. We might imagine a little twinkle in his eye and a curl in his lip in that moment of silence as he formulated his response. And then we could watch his face light up as he waited for their reaction.

Peter asked a fairly straightforward question, really. "Lord, how many times should I forgive my brother or sister who sins against me?" (Matthew 18:21). How many times, Jesus? Peter, always the pragmatist, wanted a number. He knew Jewish law. He may also have known about rabbinic teachings that held he was only required to forgive someone three times—sort of like an ancient "three strikes and you're out" rule. The only thing that matched Peter's pragmatism, however, was his impetuous zeal.

He said, "Should I forgive as many as seven times?" (verse 21).

You can almost hear in Peter's voice the kind of puffed-up motivation that blindly plagues our best intentions for forgiveness. It's as if he was saying, "Look, Jesus, I know I'm only supposed to forgive a person three times. But what if I forgive the person seven? Double the number I'm required, plus one for good measure? I bet that would make me a pretty good disciple, huh?"

Just leave it to Peter to turn the most earnest question into a self-seeking opportunity for praise.

Honestly, we can relate to him, can't we? One of the reasons we love Peter is that he is a mirror to our own souls. Let's confess for a moment how much we also are driven to forgive for the same motivations.

If I forgive this person, that will prove what a better person I am.

If I forgive someone, then surely God will be pleased with me.

Forgiveness, then, can become more an exercise in self-adulation and personal aggrandizement than anything else. Peter was really asking, "Jesus, if I forgive someone more than I'm supposed to, won't you be impressed?" We know what was in Peter's heart because, frankly, it's also in ours.

Jesus knew it, too. He knew that Peter wasn't really asking how many times he should forgive. Peter's straightforward-sounding question wasn't really so straightforward after all. Jesus could see through it. He knew Peter wasn't just asking for a number. Peter was really asking *why* he should forgive. Jesus saw in Peter's question a need to know what forgiveness is for, what it's really about. That's why he answered the question in a most odd way:

"Not just seven times, but rather as many as seventy-seven times" (Matthew 18:22). Don't forgive seven times, Peter. Forgive seventy-seven times. Or another way to understand the Greek expression is seventy times seven times—which amounts to 490 times.

To which all God's people might say, "Huh?"

Now, let's be careful with Jesus' answer. There are those who would try to interpret his answer literally. "I've got it Jesus, forgive someone 490 times. Let me break out my notebook and start keeping track."

You know there's a part of us that would do that, too. We like to keep track. We like to keep score. It would be like saying to someone, "You know what, I've got you right now at 433. By the end of the year, you're gonna be in trouble."

But to interpret Jesus' answer in that way would be to miss the point altogether. Jesus was not answering Peter's question about the number of times to forgive. Rather, he was addressing Peter's deeper question.

Why should we forgive? What should be our motivation? What, in its essence, is forgiveness?

If forgiveness is not an exercise in self-adulation, and if forgiveness is not a parlor game of keeping score, then what is it? What did Jesus really mean when he said to forgive seventy times seven times? How does this help us understand why we should forgive in the first place?

The Restoration of the World

To answer these questions, let's remember some basic background for the Gospel of Matthew. It was written in the first century AD, mostly to a community of Jewish followers of Jesus probably residing in or around the ancient city of Antioch. That means this book was written to people with a clear understanding of Jewish stories and Hebrew ideas.

Matthew's audience would therefore have been familiar with the number seven and its symbolic meanings. They would have known that seven symbolized completion or perfection. They would have known that the first and most predominant use of the number seven was in the very first story of the Hebrew Scriptures.

The first chapter of Genesis records how God created all things. How long did it take God to create light, planets, stars, trees, animals, and humans? You remember: six days. But the creation was not finished until God employed a seventh day to reflect, to enjoy creation, and to rest. It was the seventh day that brought creation to completion. It was the seventh day that brought to perfection God's work of order out of chaos. It was in the seventh day that God was finished (Genesis 1:1–2:4a).

The number seven would therefore take on special meaning in the narratives and rituals of the Hebrew people.

Every seventh day, they would be commanded to rest, observe the sabbath, and restore themselves to health (Exodus 20:8-11).

Every seventh year they would be called to give the land a rest and restore it to nourishment (Leviticus 25:1-7).

Every seventh cycle of seven years, in the year of Jubilee, they would be called to forgive debts, release slaves, and restore the land to its ancestral owners (Leviticus 25:8-13, 39-43).

The point is this: the number seven would always convey to the Israelites a sense of completion and a call to restoration, healing, and reconciliation. In the Hebrew mind, participating in the number seven would be cosmic in nature, with universal consequences. Human rest every seven days was in harmony with the created order, in which God rested on the seventh day. It involved joining together in partnership with a God who brought order out of chaos in the days of creation and is always working to bring restoration, rest, and healing out of a broken world.

Jesus' answer about forgiveness blew Peter away—not because it suggested an astronomical number of times to forgive, but because it expanded Peter's thinking about the nature and purpose of forgiveness. By saying we're to forgive seventy times seven times, Jesus showed Peter that forgiveness is about our participation in the complete restoration of all the world.

The act of forgiving someone else for an offense may feel like a private matter in a singular relationship between two individuals. But in Jesus' view, it is a sacred act with cosmic implications.

Forgiveness is full participation in the activity of God to restore all creation back to its original health, wholeness, and state of goodness. If you think forgiveness is just a small exchange between humans, think again. Whenever you forgive, you participate in God's greatest ongoing project: the restoration of the whole world back to the way it was originally intended.

That's why, in teaching us to pray, Jesus linked with the same breath the kingdom of heaven and forgiveness in the Lord's Prayer: "Thy kingdom come, thy will be done on earth as it is in heaven. Give us this day our daily bread, and forgive us our trespasses, as we forgive those who trespass against us."

Forgiveness is nothing less than kingdom-building activity.

But make no mistake. A single act of forgiveness not only helps build the kingdom of God in the cosmic, universal sense, but it can also help build God's kingdom within your own heart, mind, and spirit. And that begins with the healing that can happen in your own life.

Forgiveness and Healing

There's an emerging field over the past several years in medicine, health, and psychotherapy that explores the healing power of forgiveness. A number of studies have proven that the more one learns to forgive, the healthier one can be mentally, emotionally, and even physically.[3]

Studies have linked the ability to forgive and move past grudges to reduced blood pressure and stress levels. Being able to forgive can lead to a decrease in pain, depression, and anger in patients with chronic pain. And forgiveness therapy has led to lower levels of reported anxiety and depression among women who have been abused by a spouse.[4]

There is a link between healing and forgiveness. When you forgive, you participate in the healing of broken creation back into divine order. You also move toward a greater sense of your own healing and wholeness in your relationships.

In the end, the consequences of not forgiving are often brokenness, personal destruction, and deep sorrow.

Jim Harnish, the former senior pastor of the church where I now serve, once shared the following experience from his own ministry.

While serving his first church, he received an urgent call from a couple in the church, asking him to visit them in their house. He rushed right over with no idea as to what the issue might be. He recollects that upon entering the house, he discovered, "The house was just as joyless as they were. The anger in the room was as dark and thick as the drapes that covered the windows."

Immediately after he entered the house, the wife started to pour out the depths of her hurt and the anger she was feeling at her husband. With one vivid and painful detail after another, she described the story of how he had betrayed her by having an affair with her best friend.

After she poured out her heart and vented all of her simmering anger, Jim turned to the husband, asking him if indeed these things had happened.

"Yes," the man said. He had done it, and he had confessed it to his wife. He went on to say that he asked her to forgive him, but that she hadn't been able to do so.

Something instinctive kicked in to Pastor Jim at that moment. He turned to the couple and asked, "When did this happen?"

She snarled back. "Thirty-five years ago!"[5]

Wow. That is a long time to harbor resentment, and one can imagine the long, gradual, and deteriorating pain in that relationship. A failure to forgive over the long haul can impede the experience of God's free flow of peace, joy, and healing in a person's life.

But forgiveness doesn't have to mean to "forgive and forget." We've heard that cliché so many times we believe that forgetting is necessary if we're going to forgive. We don't recognize or account for the fact that usually, forgetting isn't even *possible*. Completely forgetting a past hurt is usually not achievable, given the way our minds work. We cannot simply erase a memory the way we can reformat a computer hard drive, or take an eraser to a chalkboard. Memories can't just disappear, and past offenses can't just evaporate.

Forgiveness also does not mean pretending that whatever happened in the past never happened. Nor does it mean that the offense is now considered okay. We don't forget harmful events or the pain that they caused.

Forgiveness, instead, involves the conscious choice to end the cycle of bitterness, revenge, and grudge-holding that is destroying your relationship with another person. It means that you will stop trying to hurt the other person for what they have done to you. Forgiveness means owning your attitudes and your actions and saying to the other person, "I choose not to hurt you anymore, regardless of what we have done to each other in the past."

Then, forgiveness means you make the conscious choice to decentralize the impact of that hurt in your life. In other words, you move the pain away from the core of who you are. Forgiveness does not mean forgetting the hurt, but it does mean deciding that you will no longer be defined by that hurt. Your emotions and your reactions will not be dictated by it. Instead of "Forgive and Forget," you will "Forgive and Decentralize." You will choose, slowly and steadily, to push the hurt away from being at the center of your life, out toward the fringe of your consciousness. It will not govern your life like it did before.

And you know as well as I do: forgiveness takes time. All of this takes time.

In the last chapter, the life and words of Thomas Merton gave us a model for how to embrace the uncertainty of doubt and disbelief. For the topic of forgiveness, I can hardly think of a more prominent and consequential figure than Archbishop Desmond Tutu, who helped lead the people of South Africa through the atrocities of apartheid and works to rebuild their society into one of freedom and love.

What does Tutu believe are the three hardest words to say? *I am sorry.* His reflections on these words tell us a lot about why we should forgive.

The Three Hardest Words to Say

In 2014, the British news agency *The Guardian* published a guest column by Desmond Tutu, in which he addressed those three hardest words to say. He began by sharing vivid childhood memories of his father's physical abuse of his mother. He remembered the smell of the alcohol in the house and on his father's breath, and he could picture the abject fear and desolation in his mother's face whenever his father would attack her. The actions of his father were as incomprehensible years later as they were when he was just a young boy, as he wondered how anyone he loved could be so inconceivably hurtful.

As a result, Tutu spent his life learning how to forgive his now-deceased father for those atrocities, and he bluntly acknowledges the difficulty in doing so. He tried to rationalize it intellectually, acknowledging his father's own pain from his background and past struggles. He tried to filter the pain spiritually, knowing that his father deserved forgiveness just as much as any of God's children—and God forgives all of us of our transgressions. But despite the intellectual understanding and spiritual conviction, Tutu came to the conclusion that forgiveness remains difficult. Such pain as he experienced stays in one's memory as a constant obstacle to forgiveness.

Such approaches are natural. We rationalize, we theologize, we access every resource we can to forgive because we know we must. Sometimes these attempts bring us back to Peter's question for Jesus because we want to know how to forgive, how long it will take to forgive, and how to make it in life until forgiveness is complete. We want the number—how many times—because forgiveness is hard and we don't want to do it one time more than we should.

Jesus' words reminded Peter that the primary question is not how or how often, but *why* we should forgive. In the same way, Tutu realized that the key to forgiveness lies not in our method but in our motivation for doing so. He said,

> Why would I do such a thing? I know it is the only way to heal the pain in my boyhood heart. Forgiveness is not dependent on the actions of others. . . . We don't forgive to help the other person. We don't forgive for others. We forgive for ourselves. Forgiveness, in other words, is the best form of self-interest.[6]

I love that last line. "Forgiveness . . . is the best form of self-interest." Forgiveness is not namby-pamby acquiescence. It is not the wimpy way out. It certainly does not advise that the victim continue to suffer abuse. Instead, it is a bold proclamation to the perpetrator that the attempts at dehumanization have failed. It is a refusal to participate in the cycle of revenge that destroys relationships and human worth. Forgiveness declares an end to mutual destruction and begins a path toward healing. In short, forgiveness is the best form of self-interest.

That's why words that seek forgiveness are, in Tutu's mind, difficult to say. "I am sorry," he writes, "are perhaps the three hardest words to say."[7] And yet they are powerful enough to set us free if we are able to say them. Words that seek and offer forgiveness allow us to orient ourselves toward an uncertain but hopeful future. As Tutu says, "It is how we free ourselves from our past errors. It is how we are able to move forward into our future, unfettered by the mistakes we have made."[8]

If you ever need a vivid example of what forgiveness looks like, then Lent points us to the cross of Jesus Christ. There you'll find the greatest model for forgiveness humanity has ever received. And thank God for it because it is in God's forgiveness of us that we discover true freedom and true healing.

Forgiveness is a difficult task. There is never a guarantee that asking for it or granting it will be easy. We may choose to forgive; it will be impossible to forget. Our minds are too keen, and our God-given memories too sharp, to ever get to a point where we'll virtually eclipse the memories of the offense. Even if we know we are supposed to forgive, it doesn't make forgiveness easy or its outcome predictable. That's what makes it so uncertain.

But we are called to forgive, nonetheless. And rather than forget, we can pray that our recollections will cease being central to our memory and move to the periphery, leaving only the details rather than the pain associated with them.

In the end, we must believe that forgiveness is not optional in the Christian life. It is a calling of the highest standard, a sacred action prompted by a divine impulse. It is God who calls us to forgive, and it is God who enables us to forgive—for the healing of the world and the healing of our souls.

Reflection Questions

1. What difference does it make for you to see the act of forgiveness as not just a private act between two people but as participation in God's grand act of restoring all of broken creation?

2. Think about times in your life when it was difficult to forgive a wrong that had been done to you. What made forgiveness hard?

3. In what ways is it difficult to forgive, not just because of what someone else has done but because of your own reluctance, inability, or misunderstanding?
4. Now think about the times when you have caused harm to someone else. Have you fully sought forgiveness for what you did? What would help in repairing that relationship with that person?
5. Finally, think about how you need to forgive yourself. What is required for you to experience the grace and mercy of God, move past your guilt and shame, and claim the life of peace that God wants for you?
6. Where is there uncertainty in the act of granting forgiveness? Where is there uncertainty in asking for or receiving forgiveness?

Embracing the Uncertain

Spend some time in prayer asking God to help you recalibrate your motivation for forgiveness. Begin by thanking God for all the ways you have been forgiven. Note any local or global stories you know that describe the power of forgiveness, and think about how they fit with God's work of restoring a broken world. Then, think about the steps you need to take today, and over upcoming days, to forgive and be forgiven by someone else.

Prayer

Gracious God, thank you for forgiving me of my sins. Empower me to follow the example you set for us in Jesus, that I might both forgive others and seek forgiveness. Help me to participate in your work to reconcile the world. Amen.

THREE

THE CROWD AND THE UNCERTAINTY OF WORRY

Read Luke 12:1-34

Somehow, the man in the crowd thought he could pull Jesus into an episode of *The People's Court*. He was in a legal dispute over the division of the family inheritance with his brother, and he, naturally, wanted Jesus to take his side.

But Jesus, often the holistic thinker when it came to earthly disputes, saw something deeper, more spiritual in the nature of the man's question. He took the opportunity to teach him, the observers, and all of us about the human propensity to worry about our possessions.

Jesus responds to the man's question with one of his better-known lessons, involving the lilies of the field and the birds of the air. Few passages in the Gospels bring comfort quite like this one. Consider the ravens; God feeds them. Consider the lilies; God clothes them. And those sparrows that cost a few coins? God keeps track of them.

If God cares for ravens, lilies, and sparrows, God most certainly cares for you.

You might have turned to this passage amid your own hard times and anguish, just as countless Christians throughout history have done. If there ever was a passage in the New Testament that rivaled the comforting power of Psalm 23 in the Old Testament, surely these verses in Luke 12 would be in the running. When we read these words, we imagine placid fields full of flowers, singing birds happily nestled in their branches, and other creatures without a care in the world because God meets their needs.

These words in Luke, and the parallel passage in Matthew, inspired songwriter Civilla D. Martin in 1905 to pen "His Eye Is on the Sparrow," one of the most famous gospel tunes ever recorded. The song, made famous by Mahalia Jackson and covered by numerous artists since, was inspired by a couple named Mr. and Mrs. Doolittle in Elmira, New York. They were both long-time sufferers of ill health, with Mrs. Doolittle essentially bedridden for twenty years and her husband confined to a wheelchair. Yet, their spirits were indefatigable, which inspired Mrs. Martin during a visit to their house.

When Martin asked the Doolittles the secret to their tenacity and courage, Mrs. Doolittle responded with a confident statement that alluded to Jesus' words in Luke 12:6: "His eye is on the sparrow, and I know he watches me." And the words to the song were born:[9]

> Why should I feel discouraged, why should the
> shadows come?
> Why should my heart be lonely and long for heaven
> and home,
> When Jesus is my portion? My constant friend is he:
> his eye is on the sparrow, and I know He watches me;
> His eye is on the sparrow, and I know He watches me.
> I sing because I'm happy, I sing because I'm free,
> for His eye is on the sparrow, and I know he watches me.[10]

Martin's lyrics offer an important reminder. Rather than long for "heaven and home," for a better time and a better place beyond the miseries and sufferings of this life, one ought to focus instead on the presence of God in the here and now, amid the struggles of today.

That is an important adjustment to make when considering this teaching from Jesus. To be comforted by God does not mean we are removed from suffering but that we are given new ways of seeing God's presence right in the middle of that suffering.

The Wider View of This Story

Remember the context of this passage in Luke's Gospel. When we widen the perspective on this text and consider the other teachings within it, we discover that these words of Jesus are not simply a kind of soothing, consoling salve for our brokenness. When we look at all of Chapter 12, we see dimensions here that we are likely to miss, which change our perception of this teaching on sparrows, ravens, and lilies.

When the chapter begins, Jesus is in the middle of a crowd of "thousands upon thousands" that had gathered so tightly they were crushing each other (Luke 12:1). In other words, this was no tranquil, seaside scene or some spacious knoll on a grassy hill. This was a congested, anguished, tension-filled, pressure-packed crowd.

Jesus begins his teaching not with soft-spoken soothing consolation but with a harsh indictment against the Pharisees. He calls out their hypocrisy, bringing to light their sinful actions and motivations that they prefer to keep hidden in the dark (Luke 12:1-3). Not exactly the best way to warm up the crowd for a comforting word.

Then Jesus reminds his listeners that following him might cost them their lives. Staying true to their commitment might get them hauled into the synagogues, before rulers and authorities, where they will need to make an account for their allegiance. They might even be killed for doing so (Luke 12:8-12). Consider those comforting words about the sparrows, that "not one of them is overlooked by God" (Luke 12:6) despite being sold for small coins. Jesus uses those words to exhort his listeners not to fear those who can kill the body, but the one who can cause suffering after death (Luke 12:4-7). It's as if Jesus takes the body's suffering as a given. If there's any notion that God's provision might mean the removal of our suffering, it's not anywhere to be found here.

After that, Jesus doubles down on the randomness and futility of clinging to life based on earthly comforts when someone asks him to help him claim his inheritance from a brother (Luke 12:13-21). The parable of the rich fool is the story of a man who was concerned with trying to immunize himself from the hardships of life by accumulating more and more possessions, only to discover that he still cannot escape death itself. "Fool!" God says to him (Luke 12:20). It's not exactly the kind of rhetoric we'd expect to set up the comforting images of ravens and lilies in the following verses, Luke 12:22-34.

And then what does Jesus say after verse 34? He offers more realistic descriptions of the darkness of the world. There is a parable of a master who comes at an unexpected hour, to observe the behavior of the unsuspecting slaves. Those who were vigilant and faithful amid their uncertainty would be rewarded, but those who disobeyed their master's wishes—believing that the master was not watching—would suffer a brutal and lethal punishment (Luke 12:42-48).

Again, the image of God there is a far cry from what we would normally associate with the comfort of ravens and lilies.

The chapter concludes with some of the most cryptic messages of Jesus: "Do you think that I have come to bring peace to the earth? No, I tell you, I have come instead to bring division" (Luke 12:51). Father vs. son, son vs. father. Mother vs. daughter, daughter vs. mother. In-laws vs. in-laws, family vs. family. Near the end of the chapter, Jesus rounds out his teaching by expanding his indictment of hypocrisy against not only the Pharisees, but also the entire crowd: "Hypocrites! You know how to interpret conditions on earth and in the sky. How is it that you don't know how to interpret the present time?" (verse 56).

So, let's review. In a matter of just one chapter, Jesus went on the offensive against the hypocrisy of the Pharisees; he told the disciples that the world would be out to kill them; he declared the futility of chasing earthly possessions; he reminded his hearers that being unfaithful and not being vigilant might bring about judgment; and he reiterated that he was here to cause division, not peace.

And right in the middle of this long diatribe, we receive words that we have too often turned into a soothing lullaby about God's comfort and care for ravens, for lilies, and for us.

When we look at Luke 12 from this high-altitude perspective, we see that the comfort of God does not transport us away from the darkness of this world but actually drills us more deeply into the midst of it. To consider ourselves as lilies and ravens does not mean that God will make life easier for us, for that may not be the case. Let's think again about Mr. and Mrs. Doolittle, who inspired Civilla Martin's hymn. God was watching them, to be sure, but Mr. Doolittle was still confined to his wheelchair, and Mrs. Doolittle remained bedridden until she died.

To receive the care of God does not mean we are lifted out of this world. Instead, it means learning to perceive God's presence and power in a new way because it might not be readily visible to our usual ways of seeing. It is not about escaping this world. It is about "interpreting the present time" and seeing God right here, with us and among us.

Alison Gopnik, a professor of psychology at the University of California, Berkeley, wrote an article in *The Wall Street Journal* with the compelling title, "When Children Beat Adults at Seeing the World." After writing her book *The Philosophical Baby*, in which she speculated that children might be more aware and observant of their surroundings than adults, she received many letters from readers supporting her claim with their own stories. One store detective described how he would observe patrons of the store from a high perch above the shopping floor. Grown-ups would be so singularly focused on the reason for their visit to the store that they never noticed him watching them from above. But their children would always glance up and wave. Unbeknownst to the adults but noticed by the children, someone up above was keeping watch over them the whole time.

Gopnik then cites a research paper in the journal *Psychological Science*, which describes a condition called "change blindness":

> You can show people a picture, interrupt it with a blank screen, and then show people the same picture with a change in the background. Even when you're looking hard for the change, it's remarkably difficult to see, although once someone points it out, it seems obvious.[11]

Ohio State University researchers Daniel Plebanek and Vladimir Sloutsky tested this theory with two sets of people: adults, and children ages four and five. After showing each group a series of colors and shapes with subtle changes in the background, they noticed that adults were better than children at focusing their attention on changes on the key shapes in the center, those objects in their "attentional spotlight," but were oblivious to subtle changes in the backgrounds of each image. Children, however, were able to see what was happening in parts of the pictures that adults were ignoring. Gopnik concludes,

> We often say that young children are bad at paying attention. But what we really mean is that they're bad at not paying attention, that they don't screen out the world as grown-ups do.... Children explore, adults exploit.... Sometimes by focusing less, we can actually see more.[12]

Gopnik's article suggests that what is important is not only what you are focusing on, but also what you are not focusing on. As you go through the harrowed busyness of your life, drowned in the competing worries and fears within and around you, are you focusing on those obvious stressors, or the more subtle yet constant presence of God in your life?

Noticing God

When Jesus talks about the comfort of God, he actually offers a challenge: to see the condition of the world in such a way that we can notice the presence, activity, and provision of God in the midst of it.

We worry about the things in our lives we cannot see. We worry about things we cannot control, and sometimes, we just worry about not being in control. Many times, we simply worry for the sake of worrying. We worry about the future. We worry about our food and our clothes. We worry about our houses and how we fit into society. We worry about what we can't see.

Jesus draws our attention to things we *can* see. Like birds and flowers, and how they don't reap or sow or feed themselves, but somehow God cares for them. Because it's not just about *seeing* what's around us, it's about **understanding** how God provides and cares for all of creation.

This text reminds us that what is important in moments of worry is getting our perspective right. It involves a change in the way we see the world, God, and ourselves.

With a few casual but critical references to flowers and birds, Jesus challenges us to shift our attention away from a future that we can't see to a present that we can see. Instead of worrying about the unknown, he is inviting us to seek the beauty of the known and God's activity in it. He calls you to see the incredible beauty and splendor of what God is doing in your life right now, which you are missing.

Essentially, Jesus calls us to exchange our crystal balls for kaleidoscopes—to stop trying to predict the future and start seeing dimensions of today that we are prone to miss. Jesus challenges us to encounter dimensions of God's love, God's grace, God's work in our lives right now in splendid, beautiful Technicolor. It's more beautiful, in fact, than flowers in a field and feathers on a bird. It's as beautiful as life itself, in all of its complexity, mystery, and glory.

There is a popular sermon illustration told of a man who was seeking the perfect portrait of peace. Not finding one that satisfied, he announced a contest to produce this masterpiece. The challenge stirred the imagination of artists everywhere, and paintings arrived from far and wide. Finally, the great day of revelation arrived. The judges uncovered one peaceful scene after another, while a gathered crowd of viewers clapped and cheered.

The tensions grew. Only two pictures remained veiled. As a judge pulled the cover from one, a hush fell over the crowd. A mirror-smooth lake reflected lacy, green birches under the soft blush of the evening sky. Along the grassy shore, a flock of sheep grazed undisturbed. Surely this was the winner.

The man with the vision uncovered the second painting himself, and the crowd gasped in surprise. Could this be peace? A tumultuous waterfall cascaded down a rocky precipice; the crowd could almost feel its cold, penetrating spray. Stormy-gray clouds threatened to explode with lightning, wind and rain.

Amid the thundering noises and bitter chill, a spindly tree clung to the rocks at the edge of the falls. One of its branches reached out in front of the torrential waters as if foolishly seeking to experience its full power. A little bird had built a nest in the elbow of that branch. Content and undisturbed in her stormy surroundings, she rested on her eggs. With her eyes closed and her wings ready to cover her little ones, she manifested peace that transcends all earthly turmoil.

The look of shock by the onlookers underscores our human tendency to only focus on the broad picture of our lives, not the subtle but steady presence of God's peace right in our midst. This is the peace that passes all understanding—peace that springs from the truth that God is powerful, and God is present.

Embracing the Uncertainty of Worry

The reminder from Jesus to consider the ravens and the lilies is a critical one for our Lenten journey, and it is possible that it is the most important reminder you need right now. It is not just to remember that God cares for you, but to actively *notice* ways that God cares for you. Then, just as plainly as you can see birds and flowers, you can pay attention to the signs of God in the present moment.

For you, embracing the uncertain might mean shifting your focus away from all those foreground pressures captivating your attention and looking for the subtle activity of God in the background. Rather than focusing on the torrent of the waterfall and the harsh spray of anxiety, notice the protective covering of God's wings that shield you even when you don't notice them.

Ultimately, this is about raising to our constant awareness the fact that when we go through the toughest struggles, we can dare to believe God is still at work. That work may not be fully revealed until later, but God is at work even in the highs and the lows of life.

We can believe that no matter what, . . . God is in our midst.

The Greeks had a word to describe this realization about time: *kairos*. It means something like the "appointed time," the idea of circumstances that are right for something. It conveys a sense of the richness and depth inherent in a given moment. It is not the kind of time that moves lifelessly onward, in a sequential march of minutes, days, and years. If we have a kairos view of time, we have a realization that each moment we have might be loaded with meaning, including caution and hope and everything in between.

Here's one more way to say it: no matter what you are going through, God is always with you. You may not be able to see that fact clearly right now. You may be going through struggles so intense that it is hard to see through the thick fog of your suffering, but that does not mean God is not here with you. God is at work, moving in ways that you may not see now.

The good news is this: God's activity is not contingent on our ability to see it. That is, after all, how God often operates: just beyond our senses and our comprehension. But take heart. Amid the cold, harsh spray of hardship, you are being cared for under God's protective, nurturing wing.

When you see that, when you realize that, then you can sing.

You are happy and free.

Reflection Questions

1. What are the ways in which you are beset with worry right now? Of those things that you are worried about, how many are things you can actually do something to change?

2. Has there ever been a time when you worried about something a great deal, only to have it work out to be better than you feared? What contributed to bringing about a better resolution than you thought?

3. Consider the words of the famous "Serenity Prayer": "God, grant me the serenity to accept the things I cannot change, courage to change the things I can; and wisdom to know the difference." How does that prayer connect to Jesus' command in this Scripture passage not to worry?

4. What can you begin to notice around you in order to help you recall God's care and provision?

5. What is the difference between peace and comfort? How can we experience peace that surpasses understanding even in the absence of comfort?

Embracing the Uncertain

Take some time to reflect in a journal about the many ways that God has provided for you throughout your life, without your seeing or acknowledging it at the time. Be thorough; think about even the tiniest blessings that you know you could not have achieved on your own or merited by your own achievement. Consider this list to be your "Lily and Raven" list, which you can refer back to (and add to) as you go through episodes of worry.

Prayer

God, I thank you that just as your eye is on the sparrow, your watchful, caring gaze is always upon me. Grant to me the ability to see in the middle of my difficulties, that I might not be so fixated on my troubles, but observant of your unfailing grace and love. Amen.

FOUR

LAZARUS AND THE UNCERTAINTY OF MORTALITY

Read John 11:1-44

I don't think there is anything that preoccupies our attention or stirs our emotions quite like our own mortality. We know, deep down inside, that none of us will make it off this earth alive, and the moment we each first realize that is a trembling experience. Whether it was during our childhoods, or in our middle-aged years, or during the twilight of our lives, we've all had moments of realization mixed with wonderment about what eternity will be like.

These are moments when we lie in bed, staring at the dark, thinking about the finiteness of life and the inevitability of death. They're moments when that part of us we'd rather ignore—the part that acknowledges that we will die—drifts into our consciousness and grips our attention.

It's that part of us that walks on the finite and imperfect side of a broken world, where bodies break down, where death still pervades, and where we find ourselves confronting the brevity of our lives. In a Lenten season that begins with Ash Wednesday's reminder that we are dust, and to dust we shall return, it is a difficult reality to ignore.

It has to be the kind of feeling that greeted Jesus when he finally decided to arrive at Bethany in John 11.

You know how the story goes. Lazarus was dying. Mary and Martha made a pitch for Jesus to come to them, but Jesus chose to wait. He didn't delay out of callous indifference to the family—in fact, we find out he truly loved Mary, Martha, and Lazarus (John 11:5, 35-36). He waited in order to make a point about God's glory (11:4). It's a point that is hard for us to hear when we are captivated by grief. But it's a point that makes all the difference in the world, and all the difference to eternity.

When Jesus arrived, Mary and Martha were grieving in the midst of their community (John 11:19). They were angry, perhaps at Jesus, but more at the unfairness of it all. And Jesus was there with them. He heard the perspective first from Martha and then from Mary that if he'd been there, Lazarus wouldn't have died (11:21-22, 32). He saw the tomb, and he shared their grief by becoming deeply disturbed and weeping (11:34-38). He spoke a word of hope to Martha (11:23-27). But he also came just to be with them, to share in their grief. Jesus was there to sit, to listen, to gather the stories and to identify with their struggles.

I have to say, of all the privileges that we as pastors observe in our profession, it is precisely moments like these, when Jesus sat with the grieving, that are our most sacred privilege.

Catching the Stories

The time I spend with a family to plan a funeral is one of the most profound aspects of ministry for me, and I imagine that's true for any pastor. Ministers serve as counselors, resident theologians, and wordsmiths at such times, in which every critical part of a clergy's calling is employed. Most of all, we are there to listen for the stories—the narratives that capture and express a family's fullest remembrance of their loved one.

Getting the stories started is fairly easy. But then the storytelling takes on a life of its own. The stories come randomly, from different members of the family, with no predetermined order or flow. Sometimes they will tell of an event from their loved one's early childhood; then the next one will be from their final days. Sometimes the accounts follow chronologically, as if following a timeline. Then on a dime, the next story will jump ahead or leap back to the past. In one moment, a family member will tell a riot of a tale that sends everyone into stitches, and then in the blink of an eye, that family member will catch a breath and become weepy.

It is like family members want to speak aloud their stories as soon as they think of them, as if sharing them out in the open will preserve them a little longer in their collective memory. I often like to think of telling and hearing these stories as catching fireflies in the night. Just tell the story, catch it, preserve it, and let its light shine, even for a moment, to brighten the darkness.

Something like that is exactly the dynamic at play when the story of Jesus and Mary and Martha takes its surprising turn. The very first thing that Martha expresses to Jesus is understandable grief and anger: "Lord, if you had been here, my brother wouldn't have died" (John 11:21). But in that same breath, in the same sentence, like a firefly at night, a new insight captures her mind. "Even now I know that whatever you ask God, God will give you. . . . I know that he will rise in the resurrection on the last day" (11:22-24). Jesus confirms her words and more: "I am the resurrection and the life. Whoever believes in me will live, even though they die" (11:25). In other words, in her grief, Martha hopes in the Resurrection, and Jesus tells her that Resurrection is standing right there in front her. He is the Resurrection and the life, and he is there.

You see, we Christian people believe that when we walk on this side of the grave, we do so in the shadow of the eternal. We claim that though we inhabit finite and mortal days, when bodies break down and death prevails, we live with the light of eternity in our hearts.

That means the power of the Resurrection and the promise of new life are not simply things that await us when we die, but they can also inform our hope and even our behavior in the way we live today. It's right here with us. He is right here with us.

Eternity can shape our mortality. The future can inform our present. The promise of God's glory yet to be revealed can actually be experienced today—so that the way we live in the present has consequences for eternity.

Despite the variety of stories that are told by family members, over the countless funerals that I have been privileged to conduct over the years, I have detected a general theme among them. Loved ones are not generally most remembered for their achievements. Or their possessions, their trophies, their financial portfolios, their number of publications, the number of zeros in their salary, or the number of abbreviations after their name.

The thing they are most remembered for? Their relationships. They are remembered for the way other people say their lives are forever changed for the good because that loved one was part of it. They are remembered for the enduring lessons of their example, the legacy of their character, and the ways that they have made those around them better people because of the love they gave.

It is not about treasures and trophies. It is about love. It's about the love we give, and receive, and give again, in the kind of reciprocal circle modeled for us in Jesus Christ. That is the only thing that lives on here on earth after we are gone.

But eventually, our minds drift back to that grand, mysterious question, the same question that Mary and Martha must have been wrestling with as they placed the sheet over their brother's face: What happens when we die?

Resurrection of the Body?

Years ago when I served in a prior church, I met with someone who reminded me of the very questions that Mary and Martha may have been pondering. She was one of the older matriarchs of the congregation. A woman who is now well into her nineties, she had lost her husband in World War II over sixty years ago. Now suffering from frail health and poor eyesight, she asked me then, "When I see my husband again, will he look like the John I remember? And will I look like the woman I am now? Will there be a sixty-year age difference? How will that work?"

I don't remember what I said exactly, except to acknowledge that ultimately it is a mystery, and that it is right to ask the questions.

This woman's questions are like those many of us wonder about. What kind of bodies will we have in the world to come? How will we recognize each other? What age will I have in heaven: the age I was when I died or a more youthful looking me? Will we see all our loved ones there? What will we do for eternity? My goodness, the questions are almost limitless, matched only by our urgency to find answers to them.

We turn to the Scriptures to discover what we can know and believe about the nature of life after death, only to find that even in the Bible, there is a wide disparity of opinions about what happens when we die.

If you look in the Hebrew Bible, the Old Testament, there are surprisingly few references to life after death. The closest we get is the concept of *Sheol*, a term often seen in the Psalms. It is a place where people go after they die, both the righteous and the unrighteous, in a state of darkness and separation from the land of the living. A select few individuals, like Elijah and Enoch, are taken up to heaven without dying in a normal sense (Genesis 5:24; 2 Kings 2:11), but there is no comment about what their existence is like after that point. Daniel 12:1-3 mentions "eternal life" for some, who will "shine like the sky...like the stars forever and always." With such ambiguous references, the Old Testament paints an unclear picture of what life after death will be like.

Skip over to the New Testament, and you get various ideas there, too. In 1 Thessalonians, Paul says that the bodies of both the righteous and the unrighteous go into the ground and stay there until the last days, when Jesus returns, and "the dead in Christ" will rise first up into the clouds to meet the Lord (1 Thessalonians 4:13-18). Until then, it seems, we're in the ground, waiting.

In the Gospels, though, as Jesus is hanging on the cross, he says to one of the criminals by his side, "I assure you that today you will be with me in paradise" (Luke 23:43). In other words, heaven is gained instantly upon death—the criminal will be in paradise *today*.

What becomes clear is that there is not one unifying voice in the Scriptures describing what our existence will be like after we die.

When we throw the traditions of the church into the mix—especially the central affirmation of the church known as the Apostles' Creed—I'm not sure if it makes matters clearer or murkier. That's because the Creed makes this point very clear: when we die, there will be a resurrection of the body. The last lines of the creed say, in no uncertain terms, "I believe in...the resurrection of the body, and the life everlasting."[13]

The Apostles' Creed does not say, "I believe in the resurrection of the spirit, or the resurrection of the soul," whatever those things mean. Many of us might have the assumption that when we die, our spirit leaves our body, or our soul ascends to heaven, leaving our body on earth. In other words, there are no bodies in heaven, only souls or spirits. But that's not what the Creed says. We believe in a bodily resurrection. A bodily resurrection? What on earth does that mean?

In the first century AD in the Roman Empire, there were some Christians who were teaching and following a set of ideas known today as Gnosticism. Gnosticism taught many things, one of which is that human beings were composed of a soul and a body. Our souls, Gnostics believed, were the divine part of us, the good part. Everything else was completely corrupted and sinful. That included all the material world, the things we could see, sense, and experience, as well as our bodies. The key to salvation for the Gnostics, then, was for the soul to escape all things material, to depart from our bodies, and to leave the material world behind. Souls, good. Bodies, bad.

One of the many problems with Gnosticism is that it therefore taught that our bodies were not worth redeeming. A Gnostic could conclude that there was no reason to take care of our bodies, or care for the earth, or care for any of the physical creation, since the goal of salvation is not to save creation, but to escape it.

But that's not what the early Christians came to believe when they looked at the whole witness of the Scriptures. They found a creation story in which God repeatedly recognizes the whole physical creation as good (Genesis 1:1-2:4a). They found an account of the Incarnation in which God's eternal Word became flesh, taking on a physical nature (John 1). With our early Christian ancestors, we believe that our bodies are gifts from God. Jesus taught that the greatest command was to love God with our entire body: heart, soul, mind, and strength (Mark 12:30). When God created our bodies in the divine image, God saw that they and the rest of the creation were "supremely good" (Genesis 1:31).

When the Apostles' Creed was formulated, it became critical to put in a clear anti-Gnostic statement that underscored that the human body, and all creation, was not bad, but worthy of resurrection. "I believe in . . . the resurrection of the body."

Our bodies are essentially good, beautiful gifts from God, and God is therefore very interested in resurrecting these bodies. It's not just our souls that exist in heaven. Somehow, we will have bodies as well.

Which leads us back to another big question, of course. What kind of body will we have?

For that answer, we turn to my favorite passage in the entire Bible that deals with life, death, and life after death. It is my go-to passage when it comes to ministering to grieving families and dealing with my own mortality.

During the course of his ministry, Paul drafted a letter to the church in Corinth—which we now know as the book of First Corinthians. At one point in the letter, he wanted to explain to the Corinthian church what kind of bodies we will have in heaven. He writes that we will not have our earthly bodies, obviously, because those will stay in the ground and decompose. But although we will have a different kind of body, it is nevertheless a very real body.

It's the same with the resurrection of the dead: a rotting body is put into the ground, but what is raised won't ever decay. It's degraded when it's put into the ground, but it's raised in glory. It's weak when it's put into the ground, but it's raised in power. It's a physical body when it's put into the ground, but it's raised as a spiritual body.

If there's a physical body, there's also a spiritual body.
                                                    (1 Corinthians 15:42-44)

Just before these verses, Paul compares our lives on earth to little seeds.

When you put a seed into the ground, it doesn't come back to life unless it dies. What you put in the ground doesn't have the shape that it will have, but it's a bare grain of wheat or some other seed.
                                                    (1 Corinthians 15:36-37)

When we die, it's like our seeds being planted in the ground. When we are resurrected to heaven, it's like the seeds sprouting into new life above the ground. Paul recognizes that the seed and the plant are very different in appearance, but in essence they are the same, and they are both essentially bodies. The seed body remains in the ground, but what sprouts is a new body that is still the same life as what was planted in the ground. You can't plant an apple seed and expect an orange tree. You can't plant soybean seeds and expect corn. The seed and the fruit contain the same essence, the same life, but they are very different expressions of it.

That, for Paul, is what resurrection of the body means. When we die, our earthly bodies stay in the ground. It doesn't matter if we are in a casket or cremated, buried in one spot or scattered. Our earthly bodies will stay on earth.

But we then sprout up into new life, with a new kind of body that is heavenly, not earthly, but still very much uniquely us and still a body in some way. Your heavenly or spiritual body will be uniquely and individually yours, with the same essence, the same life, as your earthly body. Bodies are good, and we believe in the resurrection of the body.

This poses all sorts of questions, of course, about the details of that spiritual body, many of which are similar or identical to the ones we've already asked. What age will we look like? What will that spiritual body be like? How exactly will our bodies be uniquely ours? Will we see the young, dashing Elvis, or the older, heavier one? Will all of our loved ones be there? What will heaven be like?

It's hard enough to consider the questions that Mary and Martha had to have been wrestling with when Jesus arrived. *Could this have been avoided? Why did he have to die? What are we going to do now?* These questions are tough, but when we ponder all the questions we have about what happens *after* we die, we sometimes feel at an utter and complete loss. What do we do with the uncertainty of human mortality?

Again, Paul is helpful. In 1 Corinthians 15:51, he calls life beyond death "a secret" and speaks of seeing "a reflection in a mirror" in 1 Corinthians 13:12.

There is, quite simply, a big box of things labeled "I don't know" for Paul.

But here's the important piece, the *most* important piece, actually. Just because there are things in your "I don't know" box does not mean your "I believe" box should be empty. In other words, just because we don't know all the details about our spiritual bodies in heaven doesn't mean that we don't believe in them. It just means that we don't have the evidence, the proof, the tangible earthly support for that idea that lets us identify the particulars. Jesus tells Martha that he is "the resurrection and the life" (John 11:25). Resurrection, in other words, is right there with her. And then he raises her brother from the dead to drive the point home (John 11:39-44).

Here is an important principle to embrace: if you want faith, don't look for evidence. If you want to grow in your faith, don't look for proof. If we had tangible evidence of what life would be like in heaven, then there would be no need for faith. Without faith, there would be no growth and no maturity. Faith is what stretches us, motivates us, and keeps us going. It calls you to take a risk and a leap into something unknown. It's not what's in your "I don't know" box or your "this is what I know" box that makes you grow. It's what's in your "this is what I believe" box. "Do you believe this?" Jesus asks Martha (John 11:26). Not "Do you know?" *Do you believe?* "I am the resurrection and the life. Whoever believes in me will live, even though they die. Everyone who lives and believes in me will never die" (John 11:25-26). Does Martha believe this? Do you?

Getting Ready for Another Place

The great Henri Nouwen told a story about two twins talking to each other in the womb.

> The sister said to the brother, "I believe there is life after birth." Her brother protested vehemently, "No, no, this is all there is. This is a dark and cozy place, and we have nothing else to do but to cling to the cord that feeds us." The little girl insisted, "There must be something more than this dark place. There must be something else, a place with light where there is freedom to move." Still she could not convince her twin brother.

> After some silence, the sister said hesitantly, "I have something else to say, and I'm afraid you won't believe that, either, but I think there is a mother." Her brother became furious. "A mother!" he shouted. "What are you talking about?" I have never seen a mother, and neither have you. Who put that idea in your head? As I told you, this place is all we have. Why do you always want more? This is not such a bad place, after

all. We have all we need, so let's be content."

The sister was quite overwhelmed by her brother's response and for a while didn't dare say anything more. But she couldn't let go of her thoughts, and since she only had her twin brother to speak to, she finally said, "Don't you feel these squeezes every once in a while? They're quite unpleasant and sometimes even painful." "Yes," he answered. "What's special about that?" "Well," the sister said, "I think that these squeezes are there to get us ready for another place, much more beautiful than this, where we will see our mother face-to-face. Don't you think that's exciting?"[14]

You and I often feel the squeezes that come when we confront our own mortality and our finite existence on earth. They are quite unpleasant and sometimes even painful. But God uses them to prepare us for a different sort of existence, a different kind of life: a life that is everlasting, that we can even start to experience now, if we will allow it. It's a life that begins right now, on this earth, because this world is still worth living in, still worth redeeming. You can begin living that eternal life in the way that you allow God to shape you according to God's will and as you make God's love real.

For we believe in the resurrection of the body and the life everlasting.

Reflection Questions

1. In what ways can you identify with Mary and Martha in the story? What profound and difficult questions have you ever asked of God in the wake of a loved one's death?

2. Have you ever experienced deep wrestling over your own mortality? What was the situation in which you were doing that wrestling? What gave you strength to wrestle through it, and what conclusions have you come to?

3. Think about the way you want to be remembered. Who do you know that might say that because they knew you, they were a better person?

4. What questions do you have about what things will be like after we die? How did the reflection above answer those questions, and how did it raise new ones?

5. Think about Paul's use of the seed and the plant as a metaphor for our resurrected bodies. What is helpful to you about that image? What questions do you still have?

6. Because our bodies will be redeemed and resurrected, resurrection is something that we can begin to experience in this life. What can you do today to experience a new life, a foretaste of the Resurrection?

Embracing the Uncertain

Consider making a literal list in a journal of items in your "I Believe" box and your "I Don't Know" box. What are the things that you can believe, even though you don't fully understand them? Over the next several days, pray over both lists, giving thanks to God for both the things that you are able to believe by faith and the gift of mystery that reminds us that God is greater than our comprehension. Keep referring to that list so that over time, you might see how the Holy Spirit is guiding you to embrace the uncertain.

Prayer

God, thank you for sending Jesus, who is the Resurrection and the life. Teach me to trust in you, even when I am grieving and troubled. Grant me the secure knowledge of eternity with you, even with all of my questions. Amen.

FIVE

ZACCHAEUS AND THE UNCERTAINTY OF SURRENDER

Read Luke 19:1-10

Many of us know the story of Zacchaeus for either or both of two reasons: we learned this story as children, or we heard this story in a stewardship sermon. As a child, you may have sung about Zacchaeus as the "wee little man, a wee little man was he," along with the little finger motions that pantomimed Zacchaeus scampering up that sycamore tree.

Or you probably have heard more than a handful of preachers use this story as part of a church stewardship campaign. After all, the first thing we hear about Zacchaeus is that he was very wealthy, and the last thing we hear about him is that he gave a ton of that money away. It's far too tempting a story for preachers to ignore when it comes to inviting a congregation to live into that kind of example.

But before we dwell too much on childhood memories and church finance, let's pause for a moment to ask a pretty basic question about this story: What exactly was Zacchaeus thinking when he climbed up that tree?

The truth is, we don't really know, even though we know a lot about Zacchaeus. Luke is generous to give us a veritable curriculum vitae on the man. We know his name, first of all, which is more than we can say for a lot of the people Jesus encountered. We also know his occupation, and therefore we know his reputation. As a tax collector for Rome, he not only made a living making a ton of money, but he also did it on the backs of the poor in service to the dreaded oppressors of the Jewish people. His profession made him an unpopular person.

And, of course, we know that Zacchaeus was short. There's no real reason we need to know that, except to explain why he needed to get a leg up on the crowd in order to see Jesus.

But with all we know about Zacchaeus, what we don't know is this: why exactly did he want to see Jesus?

We can speculate, of course. It's okay to do so. Whenever there is a narrative gap like this in the Scriptures, it is often the Spirit's way of inviting us to insert our own lives into the story, to fill in the gap with reasons why any of us would want to see Jesus.

Maybe Zacchaeus was searching for meaning and purpose in life, just like many of us do.

Maybe he was overcome with guilt or shame for his past misdeeds, just like many of us are.

Maybe he was just curious to get a glimpse of the man he had heard so much about, just like all of us who live in such a celebrity-obsessed culture.

We can't know for sure what Zacchaeus's reasons were, but maybe Luke gives us a hint. Consider the story that occurs right before this one.

In Luke 18:35-43, as Jesus was traveling down to Jericho, he met a blind man. Just like in the Zacchaeus story, Jesus was simply passing by. It's not the same Greek verb as what appears in Luke 19 when Jesus passes through Jericho, but the meaning is similar. That verb "passing through" in the story of Zacchaeus occurs ten times in the Gospel of Luke, more than in Matthew, Mark, and John *combined*. Clearly, the Jesus in Luke's Gospel is always on the move, and it is up to those he encounters to take notice, keep up, search for him, and get his attention.

Unfortunately for both the blind man and Zacchaeus, there was a physical impediment to seeing Jesus. The former was blind, and the latter was short. The blind man overcame his barrier by screaming. Loudly. Twice. Zacchaeus overcame his barrier by scampering up a tree. Both men needed to conquer crowds because both men wanted to see.

Now consider this. Blindness is often the Bible's way of describing a person's spiritual condition. Jesus once described people's inability to understand the deeper meaning of the parables by saying "although they see, they don't really see" (Matthew 13:13). Paul describes those who do not believe in Jesus as blinded by the god of this world (2 Corinthians 4:3-4). Even Paul's own conversion was marked by a bright light that enabled him to see the resurrected Jesus (Acts 9:1-19). Biblically speaking, sight is not just about having use of one of our physical senses. The verb *to see* in Greek contains dimensions of perceiving, knowing, and understanding. The blind man may have needed help in order to see Jesus physically. But I think Zacchaeus needed help in order to see Jesus in this other sense—in order to *know* Jesus.

That desire to know Jesus, to understand Jesus, and to become connected to Jesus was Zacchaeus's real desire deep down inside. He didn't just want to get a glimpse of him. He wasn't just wanting a favor from him. He wanted to know who this man was, and he was going to do anything he could to search for him, seek him out, and find him.

We'll get back to Zacchaeus in a bit, but I can't help but think for a moment about the other person in the Bible who longed to know Jesus this intimately, this closely. When the apostle Paul was writing to the Philippians, he said, "I want to know Christ and the power of his resurrection and the sharing of his sufferings by becoming like him in his death, if somehow I may attain the resurrection from the dead" (Philippians 3:10-11 NRSV).

These words are amazing. This is Paul, remember. If there was such a thing as a Discipleship Hall of Fame, his image would be enshrined there. Yet here he was, saying that he didn't know Jesus the way he wanted to. That may seem unthinkable, but it is also quite liberating. Maybe Paul, just like the blind man and Zacchaeus, actually gives us permission to acknowledge the uncertainty and tentativeness we feel when it comes to knowing and following Jesus. Maybe the key to faith is not being certain, but allowing faith to begin where certainty ends.

In other words, maybe it's okay to embrace the uncertain—to say, like Paul did, "I want to know Christ."

We'll visit Paul again before the end of this chapter, but let's get back to Zacchaeus.

Being Seen

As soon as he made it to the top of that tree, Zacchaeus immediately realized something. It was something that had to have surprised him, caught him off guard. As he was clinging to that tree trunk, digging in his nails and flexing his forearms to hold on for dear life, he noticed that just as he was straining to catch a glimpse of Jesus . . .

. . . Jesus was already looking at him.

This is another similarity between Zacchaeus and the blind man in Luke 18:35-43. Despite all the shouting and tree climbing, and despite all the efforts they each made to seek Jesus out, Jesus was already returning the favor. He said to the blind man, "What do you want me to do for you?" (Luke 18:41). He said to Zacchaeus, "Come down at once. I must stay in your home today" (19:5). In both cases, it was like Jesus was saying, "Look, friends, let's get right down to business. Let's skip the pleasantries and move beyond the fact that you've been looking for me. I, in fact, have had my eye on you, and I am here to help."

John Wesley was so taken with this idea that God is the one who searches us out, rather than the other way around, that he developed an important contribution to the theology of Methodism called *prevenient grace.* It is the grace that goes before us, before we are even able to recognize it or understand it, which has been at work in our lives since the moment we were born. It is never static, always on the move, always luring us, wooing us, searching for us, and drawing near to us.

In other words, in the fashion of Luke's Gospel, it is the grace of God that is constantly *passing through* our lives.

Even though we long to see Christ and discover an intimate relationship with the God who created us, we are surprised to find out that this God has actually been searching us out the whole time. God stands there, in the midst of the crowd, looking us square in the face, and asks, "What do you want me to do for you?" As we are pulling, straining, climbing, and inching our way up toward God's attention and favor, God is standing there the whole time, saying, "Okay, alright, friend. Stop climbing. You're only going to hurt yourself. Get down. I've come to you. Let's enjoy some dinner."

Yes, we often like to skip ahead into the story of Zacchaeus and get to the part where he sells his goods and gives the proceeds to the people he cheated. That's certainly the fruit of the encounter. But before any of this happened, let's not miss the fact that Jesus not only noticed him; Jesus had drawn near to him, and he took the initiative to develop a relationship with Zacchaeus on his own terms.

Zacchaeus may have wanted to *see* Jesus, but the power of this story is that he was *seen* by Jesus. He wanted to *know* Jesus, and found that he was *known* by Jesus.

What Jesus saw in Zacchaeus was a man ready to be changed. Zacchaeus had been struggling with his burdens for so long that as soon as Jesus saw him, he was prepared to do whatever it took to be anything other than he was: an unethical cheat.

When Jesus looked at him with kindness and compassion, Zacchaeus knew that the time for repentance and transformation had arrived. There would be no more delay. There would be no reason to wait. There was no indication that things would get any better next week than they were last week, unless he responded to Jesus' invitation.

Get down off that tree, Zacchaeus. Your time has come.

Even before Jesus arrived at his house, Zacchaeus became a changed man. He discovered that it was possible by the power of God revealed in Jesus to reverse the course of his wayward life, to undo his cheating ways, to make restitution for his wrongs, and to become a benefactor rather than a swindler.

For Zacchaeus, seeing Jesus—and being seen by Jesus—was a chance at a fresh, new start.

Just like it can be for you.

Jesus is calling you out of your tree. God is inviting you to come down so that you can be lifted up. Jesus is beckoning you into a fresh awareness of God's love for you and the fact that God has been searching for you, watching you, long before you realized it.

That realization leads to such a transformation.

Two Stories of Transformation

There are two people I think of when I think of lives transformed in the manner of Zacchaeus. The first is Archbishop Anthony Bloom, who was a Russian Orthodox monk and author of a book called *Beginning to Pray*. Like Zacchaeus, he discovered that freedom in the kingdom of God is not contingent on riches, but on love: love of others and love of God. Listen to the way he describes the freedom that comes from surrendering one's full life over to God. He begins with a question, exploring the correlation between richness in wealth and poverty of spirit:

> Have you never noticed that to be rich always means an impoverishment on another level? It is enough for you to say, "I have this watch, it is mine," and close your hand on it, to be in possession of a watch and to have lost a hand. And if you close your mind on your

riches, if you close your heart so that you can keep what is in it safe, never to lose it, then it becomes as small as the thing on which you have closed yourself in.[15]

But what was true for Zacchaeus is true for all of us: once we discover the impotence of possessions to provide the joy and peace that only God can provide, we find ourselves on the verge of true liberation, true life:

> Now if that is true, the moment you reach rock bottom, the moment you are aware of your utter dispossession of all things, then you are on the fringe of the kingdom of God, you are nearly aware that God is love and that He is upholding you by His love. And at that point you can say two things simultaneously. You can pray out of your utter misery, dereliction and poverty, and you can rejoice that you are so rich with the love of God.[16]

Zacchaeus discovered that being rich by the world's standards is nothing compared to being "rich with the love of God."

The other person I think of when I think of Zacchaeus-like transformation is Richard Graves, an eighteenth-century American Methodist whose spiritual life had descended into complacency. He had been a Christian for over twenty years, yet he realized it had been a very long time since he felt a strong connection and intimacy with God. He was longing to *see* God, and he was willing to do anything to experience it. "The language of my heart was, 'Give me love or else die,'" he wrote in his journal. "For near four weeks I felt such keen pain within, that I could almost say, I prayed without ceasing, but with little joy."[17]

And then, a breakthrough:

> It was on Monday, the second day of July 1799, that the Lord poured down his blessing into my heart.

In the evening my happiness increased till I went to bed, with raptures of joy unknown.... In a few days my rapture of joy abated, and I had some temptation and struggle. Not that I had any reason to doubt of the work being wrought, but if it was consistent with such a work of grace for me to have such feelings, but I soon discovered the device of the enemy to rob me of my confidence, and the Lord multiplied my peace. I now, notwithstanding temptations, feel the abiding witness. My mind is stayed on God. Christ is my object. I am willing to take him for my portion. He is the fairest among ten thousand. He is altogether lovely.[18]

That remarkable moment of transformation took place in 1799, when Graves was eighty-five years old. It happened after decades of him being a minister himself, and a mere five years before he died.

If it wasn't too late for Graves to renew his passion for God, it's not too late for you.

Which brings us back to the apostle Paul.

Paul says to the Philippians, "I want to know Christ and the power of his resurrection" (Philippians 3:10 NRSV). If Christ wasn't raised from the dead, then the Christian story is a failure, in which God fails to win our love back. But if Christ is raised from the dead, then God's love is not finally in vain, our love is not finally in vain, and all that is done for love will finally become fruitful.

Death does not have the final word; hope really is the shape of tomorrow. All our pain and shame and regret will in the end be redeemed because nothing is wasted forever. If Christ is raised, we can be sure that fear will pass away and joy will prevail. All will at last become beauty.

That's the only power that matters in the end. Financial power, military power, nuclear power—no power can compare with this. The power of resurrection is the power that dismantles every other power.

When Paul says "I want to know Christ," he says he wants to know this power, the power of resurrection.

Paul is saying that he doesn't just want to be the beneficiary of Jesus' resurrection. He wants to identify with that resurrection so that in acknowledging the deepest, darkest realities of his broken human condition, he can experience the overwhelming love of God that can transform him into new life.

Just like Zacchaeus climbed that tree in order *see* Jesus, Paul wanted to *know* Christ. What they both found was that Jesus had already seen and known them. Just like Jesus called Zacchaeus to come down, Jesus raised Paul up, through the power of resurrection.

Knowing Christ is knowing the power of his resurrection. The ultimate question for you during the remainder of this Lenten season might be this: how is Jesus calling you down from that tree, so that you can be lifted up into resurrection?

Reflection Questions

1. Describe a time in your life when you were seeking after God, to get some fuller understanding of who God is to you.
2. Have you ever come to a realization that God has been working in you without your acknowledging it? If so, what was that experience like? How had God been working within your life?
3. If Jesus were to call you down from a tree and invite himself over for a meal with you, what kinds of conversation topics would you want to cover? What changes in your life do you think Jesus would ask of you?
4. Consider Paul's desire to want to know Christ and the power of his resurrection. In what ways are you longing to experience the Resurrection today? How might you pray that God might reveal that power to you? What are you willing to give up so that you can experience that power?

5. How do you feel a need to be seen and known by God?
6. How do you think God is seeking you, searching for you, looking at you right now? How do you know?

Embracing the Uncertain

Spend some moments in silence every day over the upcoming week. Target at least fifteen minutes, or whatever is most feasible for you. During that silence, find a centering word or phrase that you can use to refocus your silence whenever your mind starts to drift. You might choose a word or phrase from this story of Zacchaeus, or the words of Paul, such as "I want to see Jesus," or "I want to know Christ," or "I want to welcome Jesus." After those periods of silence, reflect in a journal what changes God might be calling you to make in your life.

Prayer

God, thank you for seeking me out, even as I have longed to see you. Lead me into a deeper experience of the death and resurrection of Jesus, that I might know your power and live the life you wish for me to live. Amen.

SIX

JESUS AND THE UNCERTAINTY OF OBEDIENCE

Read Matthew 26:36-46

Our Lenten journey now enters the most important week of the
Christian year, in which we follow Jesus through the city gates on
Palm Sunday and walk with him along the dusty, well-worn path that
will lead to a hilltop cross. Most of the stories we encounter during
Holy Week concentrate on Jesus and his interaction with one or more
individuals, but not this one. Here, the focus is on Jesus' interaction
with the Father. On the night before he died, after his last meal with
his friends and with his closest associates slumbering naively in the
background, Jesus is all alone in the garden of Gethsemane, pouring
his heart out to God with deep sadness and distress.

At the core of his prayer is this cry of anguish: "My Father, if it's
possible, take this cup of suffering away from me. However—not what
I want but what you want" (Matthew 26:39). By the time his torture
and death are over, he will feel isolated, abandoned, and longing to
hear God's voice.

It could be that while each of the first five sessions in this book has
resonated with you and your current spiritual condition in some way,

this story may be the one you identify with the most. For there may be no more difficult moment in our faith journey than when we find ourselves unable to hear God's voice, discern God's will, and turn our full life over in surrender.

You may have heard this story. For heaven's sake, you may have *lived* this story before:

A man went to his doctor.

"I think my wife's going deaf," he told the physician.

"Try to test her hearing at home and let me know how severe her problem is before you bring her in for treatment," the doctor said.

So, that evening, when his wife was preparing dinner, the man stood fifteen feet behind her and said, "What's for dinner, honey?"

No response.

He moved to ten feet behind her and asked again.

No response.

Then he stood five feet behind her and tried again but still got no answer. Finally, he stood directly behind her and asked, "Honey, what's for supper?"

She turned around. "For the fourth time—I said chicken!"

Ah, it seems that many of us will have hearing trouble at some point in our lives, maybe without even realizing it. That's not the real news. The real news is the degree to which all of us—all of us—have had trouble in some point in our lives with hearing God.

We have all been there, laboring over a decision, struggling with feeling alone, wondering if God really is out there and really listening. We've heard time and again from lots of preachers that the problem is not whether God is speaking to us, but whether we have done enough to listen to God. We begin to doubt God and ourselves, unsure about which of us has the hearing problem. All we know is that we're experiencing divine silence.

We wish we could "hear" God, the way Abraham or Noah could. We wish we could "see" God the way Moses or Elijah could. We wish we could interact with Jesus the way the Peter or Mary Magdalene could. We want to encounter God directly, with our physical ears, with our eyes, or in a real face-to-face conversation. We'd even settle for seeing the scars, the way Thomas could.

Wouldn't the life of faith be a whole lot easier? A whole lot more certain? With much less doubt? Wouldn't we be able to do what God is asking us to do with a lot more conviction if we could hear God's voice as surely as we can hear another person talking?

But when you think about it, if a less certain kind of faith were not necessary, how would we grow?

If we didn't have to crane our necks, hone our ears, and hush the noise of the world around us, then we wouldn't mature, wouldn't emerge from difficult times stronger and more faithful than we were before. Learning to listen can be painful, difficult, and bewildering, especially in those times when we feel hopeless and alone. But even the act of learning to listen, of trying to listen, is itself a blessed practice that can make you a stronger Christian.

Palm Sunday and the Annunciation

I do not think it is a coincidence that every Lenten season there is a close proximity between two biblical commemorations.

The first event is March 25, known as Annunciation Day. It is precisely nine months before Christmas Day, and it celebrates the visit by the angel Gabriel to a young Mary, in which she was told that she would give birth to the Messiah.

The second event is Palm Sunday and the start of Holy Week, in which we once again travel the dark, desolate path that ends with the cross on Golgotha. I never realized it until recently, but even though the date of Palm Sunday moves around from year to year, these two events are always within proximity of each other—they're never more than a month apart and usually occur within two weeks of each another. There was likely no intentionality behind scheduling the two so closely, but theologically, considering them together makes a profound statement about the nature of Christian obedience.

If there is anything we admire about Mary, it was her willingness to say yes to God. She put her life at risk when she chose to bear God's Son. Her fears and doubts would have made it quite understandable for her to choose the easier path of self-preservation. Instead, she chose to obey God, regardless of the cost and pain that were sure to follow.

Thirty-three years later—but only a matter of days in liturgical time—we find a similar scene in the garden of Gethsemane. Here the son of Mary wrestled with the very same kinds of questions that his mother faced when he was conceived. He had a choice between comfort and obedience, between self-preservation and self-sacrifice, between human will and God's will.

By linking together Annunciation Day and Palm Sunday, we can draw parallels between these bookends of the life of Jesus. He was born of a woman who chose to obey God at all costs, and he chose to live that same life of obedience until the very end.

We might even imagine Jesus, as a very young boy, learning this important life lesson about obedience from the one who learned it herself at a very young age.

"Mother, tell me the story again of how the angel visited you," he might ask.

"Well, dear, he caught me by surprise one day," Mary would respond, beginning the tale just like she had in countless prior retellings. "He told me not to be afraid, and that God had chosen me to give birth to you."

"Were you afraid, Mother?"

"I was at first, of course. Nothing like this had ever happened to me, and I didn't know what others might think. But there was something about the presence of God in that angel that gave me great comfort. I said yes, and I'm so glad that I did."

"Why were you glad, Mother?"

"Because then I could have you in my life, son! But more than that, I knew deep down in my heart that God was going to do great things to change the world, and that God wanted to do them through me. To exalt the humble, feed the hungry, remember the lowly: it is a privilege to be used by God in such a powerful way. We must say yes, even when it is difficult to do so. Do you understand, son?"

"Yes, Mother. May I ask another question?"

"Of course, dear."

"Can you sing me that song again? The one you sang when you said yes to the angel?"

As Jesus was praying in the garden of Gethsemane, he was straining his ears to hear his Father's voice and wrestling with whether he would follow through on the very reason he came to earth. Would he be obedient to God's purposes, or would he cower away in fear? He would gladly let this cup pass from him, but he just wanted to do his Father's will.

I like to imagine that in that moment, the words of his mother's Magnificat entered his mind (Luke 1:46-55). In those moments when life is most difficult, and the pain and trauma of life have us squarely in their crosshairs, we tend to have our sharpest and clearest memories of the lessons our parents taught us. We tend to recall lessons about staying steadfast in our convictions, unwavering in our principles and courageous in our actions. We learn from our ancestors how to claim our future. I think Jesus learned a thing or two about obedience from the woman whose obedience brought him into earthly existence.

Jesus once said that if you want to gain your life, you must be willing to lose it, and that only those who lose their life would eventually find it (Matthew 16:25). You and I have that same choice today, and we have two role models to lead the way.

A mother and her son.

It's the same choice, by the way, that each of the disciples had to make. They all chose the way of self-preservation rather than the path of obedience. We know the story of Holy Week. We know how it begins and how it ends. It begins with the crowds, including the disciples, all on the side of Jesus. The crowds were filled with people who were waiting with eager anticipation for the arrival of their liberator, their king, their messiah. Jesus, in their minds, could do no wrong.

But as every day of Holy Week passed by, there would be fewer and fewer people by his side. The first was Judas. We know about him; he began to fall away first, lured perhaps by the greed of money or maybe by disappointment in Jesus. We don't know what drove him; we just know he abandoned Jesus. We think to ourselves, surely the others would not fall away.

But they did.

Matthew, James the Lesser, Andrew, Bartholomew, Thomas, Simon. One by one, they fell away. By the time he reaches the garden of Gethsemane, Jesus is alone with the inner circle, Peter, James, and John.

It appears Jesus had called these men together because they were the ones he felt would have been most loyal to him during this time of need. If anyone should have gotten the point of Jesus' mission on earth, it should have been these three. If anyone should have known what it would mean to be obedient, to lose their lives to gain them, it should have been them. He asked his friends to stay awake with him and keep alert (Matthew 26:37-38).

But the disciples could not even do that. When given the choice to stay vigilant and loyal or to give in to their fatigue and their slumber, they chose to sleep—to fade away in peace and comfort. Even when Jesus directly told Peter, James, and John why it was important to him that they stay awake (for he was deeply grieved, even to death), the disciples chose to disobey (Matthew 26:38-40).

Although the disciples aren't as fickle as the crowds on Palm Sunday turn out to be, in the garden of Gethsemane they show that their commitment to Jesus isn't firm enough. The disciples too will leave Jesus to suffer alone. This connection between the crowds at Palm Sunday and the disciples in the garden of Gethsemane challenges us to see our own tendency to fall away from Jesus. Like the crowds and the disciples, we always have a choice: whether to listen for God's voice and do what is difficult, or choose the more comfortable path. Like water running downhill, we will always tend to choose the path of least resistance.

We will choose to follow Jesus, as long as he meets our own expectations.

We will choose to identify with Christ, so long as it is convenient.

We will stay alert and awake in our prayers, so long as fatigue and hunger do not overtake us.

We will stand by Jesus' side, until the risk becomes too great.

Beginning with the crowds of Palm Sunday, and then the band of twelve disciples, and finally including his closest friends of all, each person chose the wider path and fell away from Jesus.

All that we have left is this one, Jesus, who chose to confront his innermost fears and follow the more difficult, more resistant way. It was a path that would lead him to a cross, to certain death. Yet that was the only way that would eventually lead to life. For as Jesus said, if you want to gain your life, you have to lose it.

So, here is the question that compels us this Holy Week: what kind of path will we follow?

Here we are, on this Palm Sunday, celebrating the arrival of this Jesus. Will we choose to follow only the Jesus we are comfortable with, the one who comes to meet our needs and fulfill our expectations, or will we allow him to lead us into the difficult, uncertain places of surrender, self-sacrifice, and obedience?

What are the areas in your life in which you have, for too long, chosen the path of least resistance? By refusing to engage the difficult and the uncomfortable, when or how have you given in to the easy and the temporary? Maybe you have given in to

- the temptations that have controlled you,
- the guilt and shame that have haunted you,
- the bias and prejudice that have warped your thinking,
- the resentment and bitterness that have blocked your ability to forgive,
- the self-centeredness that has kept you from truly using your gifts and your time to make a difference,
- the anxiety that has blocked the free flow of God's joy.

Or maybe you've given in to something else. Whatever it is, take a lesson from the Palm Sunday crowds. It is time to realign your will and your actions with those of Jesus, who comes not to meet your expectations but to call you out of your comfort zone.

Take a lesson from the disciples. It is time to wake up from your slumber and enter the difficult task of following Jesus, no matter the cost.

Take a lesson from Mary herself, who chose to be obedient to God regardless of the cost; who sang a song of obedience, a song that perhaps Jesus heard in his own mind as he prayed in the garden that night:

> *With all my heart I glorify the Lord!*
> *In the depths of who I am I rejoice in God my savior.*
> *He has looked with favor on the low status of his servant.*
> *Look! From now on, everyone will consider me*
> *highly favored*
> > *because the mighty one has done great things*
> > *for me.*
> *Holy is his name.*
>
> *(Luke 1:46-49)*

Let's face it. Realigning our will, waking up from our spiritual slumber, and choosing to be obedient to God takes initiative, constant attention, and the gracious work of the Holy Spirit. It also requires regular spiritual discipline, centered on the practice of hearing God's voice, and learning to surrender and trust.

Hearing God

I want you to know that if you are having trouble hearing God, there is good news. Simply your desire to hear, and your efforts to listen to God, are pleasing to God. And that desire to please God is, in fact, pleasing to God.

Here is a simple, practical set of principles for how you might be able to listen for God's voice. You can use the familiar acronym "S.O.S." whenever you need to send up a flair amid troubled times. But I don't want to suggest that you use these principles only when you are in trouble.

The practice of listening for God's voice needs to be cultivated regularly as part of a lifelong pattern. Indeed, if you only use S.O.S. when you are in trouble, it would be like trying to run away from a wild animal when you've been sitting down for days in a row. Stiff muscles, unused to exertion, will not function as well as they could with regular stretching and training. In the same way, using S.O.S. in times of crisis will be harder, more painful, and even potentially injurious unless you begin practicing these behaviors now.

Scripture

The first letter is S. That stands for Scriptures. It is in the Bible that you can listen for the word of God at work in your life, hearing the guidance, comfort, and encouragement that resonate with your difficulties and give you confidence about your future. In my toughest moments, I have turned to familiar Scriptures that have carried me through in the past. I encourage you also to return to the Scriptures as a source of solace.

Begin now a daily pattern of reading from the Scriptures. Mark your Bibles with words and insights that you glean from them. Write in a journal your reflections on the Bible, and keep it as a daily record of what God is telling you. The Bible is a gift to us from God, a complete and accurate record of what God has said to faithful people in the past.

Others

The O stands for others. You must surround yourself with thoughtful, prayerful people you can trust. Select people in your life who have your best interest at heart, even if it means that they might tell you things you might not want to hear. Sometimes, the word that

God wants to tell us is troubling, and our own pride or stubbornness prevents us from being open to hearing something we want to avoid.

Turn to others you trust for their advice, and at times, even invite from them brutally honest words that you might not want to hear. God will use pastors, parents, friends, family, professionals, and sometimes even strangers to lead you. Always check what they say against the words of Scripture, but don't be afraid to lean on the words of others for guidance.

Silence

Finally, the second S stands for silence. Create moments—or better yet, a daily pattern—of quiet to pray and listen for God. Ask God, first of all, to silence all other voices in your mind except the one that belongs to God.

Prayer sometimes means talking and listening to God even though you are not sure if anyone is listening or speaking on the other end. Sometimes, prayer means "talking in the dark," as my professor and author friend Steve Harper likes to say. It means saying prayers unsure if they are really doing any good. But know this: every time you pray— every time—it is doing good. God is listening, and the act of quieting your heart and mind to listen for God will open your life up to new possibilities, insights, and guidance.

As we round the corner through Holy Week and head toward the glory of Easter morning, let us take heart. Jesus gives us the model for opening our ears to sense God's voice, opening our minds to surrender to God's will, and opening our hearts to give ourselves for others. It is not easy; there will be competing voices within us and around us, much the like Palm Sunday crowds who would drown out God's voice with their own.

But as these final days go by, as we are drawn into the drama and passion of Maundy Thursday and Good Friday, we can quiet our spirits, silence all voices but God's alone, and sit in the garden with Jesus, praying to God, "Not what I want, but what you want."

Reflection Questions

1. When has there been a time in your life when uncertainty has caused your faith to stretch and mature?
2. When have you ever longed to hear God's voice?
3. Have you ever experienced silence from God? Did it feel more like God wasn't speaking or that you weren't hearing?
4. Consider again the connection between Holy Week and Annunciation Day. Who are the people who have influenced you during formative times of your life, and whose impact continues to shape the choices that you make today? How might you acknowledge them, even thank them personally, or at least give thanks to God for them?
5. How have you heard God's voice or discerned God's will in the past through Scripture, through others, or through silence?
6. What changes do you need to make in order to surrender to God and obey God more completely?

Embracing the Uncertain

During this Holy Week, participate in both the Maundy Thursday and Good Friday services in a church near you. During Holy Saturday, find some quiet time to pray for the people you know. Make a list of family members, friends, and others, and say a prayer for each one, lifting up any concerns you know of that they are facing. If you are on social media, say a brief prayer for every one of the people you are connected to. Finally, spend some time in prayer asking for God to reveal to you how you might give of yourself, sacrificially, for those people in need.

Prayer

God, thank you for calling me to obedience. Forgive me for not always hearing your voice. Accept my desire to hear you as itself an offering of obedience. Lead me to a place of surrender, that I might experience the joy of the Resurrection in Jesus. Amen.

SEVEN
THE EMPTY TOMB AND THE PROOF OF THE RESURRECTION

Read Matthew 28:1-7; Mark 16:1-8;
Luke 24:1-12; and John 20:1-18

Given the diversity of perspectives among the four Gospel writers, it should not be surprising to hear that there are only a handful of miracle stories that all of the Gospels have in common. It should also not be a surprise to hear that the resurrection of Jesus is one of them.

Yet, each writer tells the story in his own unique way. By comparing their versions to one another, we can discover how each Gospel writer answers the question, "In a world of uncertainty, how can we be sure that the Resurrection is real?"

Let's face it. The idea of a physical resurrection of a dead person back to life is an utterly irrational claim to make. Many of us are far too empirical, and far too skeptical, to readily believe that the resurrection of Jesus actually happened. But as people of faith, we believe not only that the Resurrection *happened*, but also that it is the central aspect of our Christian conviction. Without the Resurrection, there would be no Christianity.

How do we get past our skepticism and find a way to claim that the Resurrection is real? When we take a look at how each Gospel writer answers that question, we not only find a way to *believe* that the Resurrection was real, but we also discover that the power of resurrection is still at work today.

Matthew: Go See Him for Yourself! (Matthew 28:1-7)

Mary Magdalene and the other Mary knew what had happened to Jesus. Little more than thirty-six hours had passed since he died on that cross and was buried, so the news was still fresh in their minds. There would be no possible way for them to expect the events that greeted them when they arrived at the tomb.

An earthquake. An angel, glimmering like lightning and white as snow, descending from heaven. The giant stone, rolled away.

We know what these events mean. Many of us have lived through too many Easter mornings and heard the gospel message too many times not to know what happened when the women arrived. They were firsthand eyewitnesses to the greatest miracle in human history. They were the first to see the Resurrection. Death had been defeated, despair turned to glory, and the bad news flipped on its ear to make way for the best news of all.

However, . . .

Notice that even though the women had witnessed the Resurrection, they were still not *affected* by it. Even though they were eyewitnesses to the good news, they were not yet living into the good news. We know this because the angel had to tell them not to be afraid, and not to dwell too much on what this scene all meant. "Don't be afraid. I know that you are looking for Jesus who was crucified," the angel told them, acknowledging that they were still confused by what they had seen (Matthew 28:5). Then he tells them what happened: "He isn't here, because he's been raised from the dead, just as he said" (28:6).

Notice what the angel does here. He recognizes the women's fear and their anxiety. He acknowledges the fact that even though they saw the Resurrection happen, they did not yet know what it meant. Then he tells them, simply and directly, that Jesus has been raised from the dead. The angel doesn't even attempt to explain how the Resurrection happened. No word about how a body that had died could come back to life, how a brainwave that had gone flat could be jump-started again, or how cells that had been in rigor mortis could be stirred back into action.

The angel chooses to say nothing about how the Resurrection happened but instead just tells them as clearly as possible *that* it has happened. Then he invites them to go meet the resurrected Jesus.

We can easily get so caught up with more bad news than we can handle that we might not know what good news looks like, even if we witness it firsthand. The reality is, God is resurrecting dead things to life all the time, all around us. Yet we are so locked in on our fears and anxieties that we miss it.

So the very next words of the angel to the women are precisely the same words that Matthew believes you and I need to hear today:

> *"Now hurry, go and tell his disciples, 'He's been raised from the dead. He's going on ahead of you to Galilee. You will see him there.' I've given the message to you."*
> (Matthew 28:7)

In other words, the angel tells the women, "Look, don't just stand there trying to figure out what to make of this good news. If you do, you're going to miss it, and you won't understand it anyway. Instead, get up, get going, get moving, get active, and go see this Jesus for yourself."

Here is Matthew's Easter advice, in a nutshell:

- If you are not in a place in your life where you can believe in the Resurrection, then start practicing it until you *can* believe it.

- If you are struggling in your prayer life, with doubts about its nature and whether it is effective, keep praying until you *can* believe it.
- If you have a strained relationship with your Bible, wrestling over its words and even struggling to read it at all, then keep on reading it, every day, for the Holy Spirit will guide you until you *can* believe it.
- If you have had a bittersweet relationship with the church, have been betrayed by the Christian community in the past, and are reluctant to make church attendance and participation a part of your life, then keep on showing up, regularly, until you *can* believe it.
- If you have questions about God's presence in the midst of suffering, then look for God's presence in the midst of your own.
- If you have real fears about being abandoned by a God you are not sure even exists, then join arm and arm with someone whose belief can buoy your own until you can accept it for yourself.

In other words, if you doubt the Resurrection, then start practicing resurrection—living a life that counts on the Resurrection—until you can believe the Resurrection for yourself.

That is exactly what the angel told the women. Go to Galilee. You may still have your doubts and may still be afraid. And who can blame you? But God is calling you to do something about it. Get active in your faith. Go meet this resurrected Jesus.

Mark: Both Late and Early (Mark 16:1-8)

If you've ever seen a live Passion play, you've probably seen the usual visual effects when it gets to the Easter story. Something funny happens with the lights. There's a loud noise. Maybe a rush of wind or a burst of blaring trumpets. Then suddenly, thanks to some theatrical magic, the rock that sealed the entrance of the tomb mysteriously rolls out of the way!

That's the usual sequence of events in live Passion plays. But it's not what happens in Mark's Gospel.

In Mark, nobody sees the Resurrection happen: "When they looked up, they saw that the stone, which was very large, had already been rolled back" (Mark 16:4 NRSV).

Did you catch that? The stone was *already* gone. It was a past tense event!

But here's something else. Matthew and John each record a meeting between the women and Jesus. It happens shortly after they've been told about the Resurrection (Matthew 28:8-10; John 20:11-18). The most famous account of this is when Mary Magdalene meets Jesus at the tomb and thinks he's the gardener (John 20:11-18). But nothing like this happens in Mark's Gospel.

The women were not only too late to experience the Resurrection, but they were also too early to meet the resurrected Jesus:

> *Going into the tomb, they saw a young man in a white robe seated on the right side; and they were startled. But he said to them, "Don't be alarmed! You are looking for Jesus of Nazareth, who was crucified. He has been raised. He isn't here. Look, here's the place where they laid him. Go, tell his disciples, especially Peter, that he is going ahead of you into Galilee. You will see him there, just as he told you."*
>
> (Mark 16:5-7)

In Mark's Gospel, the meeting between the women and Jesus takes place after the final curtain closes, if it happens at all. The implication is that Jesus has gone ahead of them, and they are to continue moving forward in order to meet him. In other words, in Mark, God's power and presence had preceded the women in the act of resurrecting Christ and had also gone before them in the presence of the resurrected Christ.

In one seemingly ordinary moment in time, at a place where the women came to the tomb expecting to find death and despair, they came to realize that not only was God with them in the present moment, God was working clearly in their past and already preparing their future.

In Mark's Gospel, resurrection is presented as that which God has done, is doing, and will always do.

The power of the Resurrection through Christ is nothing less than the power to redeem the haunting guilt and shame of our yesterdays, the ongoing sufferings and despair of today, and the anxieties and worries of tomorrow. The message of the cross is comprehensive. It is thorough, it is timeless, and it is time-altering.

If any of this sounds to you remotely resonant with John Wesley's understanding of grace, then I think you're on to something.

God has worked in our past, in ways that we are not fully aware of, luring us into a relationship with God, injecting our lives with little glimpses of grace. There have been unexpected moments when God spoke to us, loved us, and cared for us, in effect rolling away the stone for us, even before we realized it. This is called prevenient grace. It is the grace that God gives to us even before we know it.

God is working in our present. The power of the Resurrection leads us to a place of utter humility and obedience to God, to the point where we are left with no response but to surrender ourselves wholly to the one who raised Jesus from the dead. Through the Resurrection, we can experience new life today. This is the justifying, saving grace of God, available to everyone. Accepting that grace will lead to an experience of new life and new freedom.

God is working on our future. God is molding you, shaping you, and preparing you for the destiny God desires for you. God will journey with you into the vast depths of unknown tomorrows, showing you how your talents and abilities will contribute to the wider plan of God's kingdom. God's resurrection guarantees our future security. This is the sanctifying grace of God.

John Wesley believed that the grace of God comes before us, goes before us, and lives with us still. That's what the women at the tomb experienced firsthand. The Resurrection had happened. The resurrected Christ awaited them. The Resurrection experience was real.

Luke: Between Two Memories (Luke 24:1-12)

What is interesting at the outset of Luke's version of the Easter story is that we are not given the names of the women. At least not yet.

Much of the opening of the story is resonant with the other Gospels. The women showed up to do their job, to prepare the body of Jesus with spices and do their due diligence. When they arrived at the tomb, they saw the stone had already been rolled away, and two brightly dressed men were standing there to tell them, "Why do you look for the living among the dead? He isn't here, but has been raised" (Luke 24:5-6).

Like in the other Gospels, the women react with understandable fear. The news that they received disrupted their normal pattern of expectations. Dead things are supposed to stay dead; hopelessness stays hopeless; and darkness stays dark. When you are looking for new life, you don't find it in the grave.

Just as we are about to chalk up Luke's Easter story as identical to the others and live with the kind of confusion and fear that the women surely felt in that moment, Luke offers the first unique curveball to his version of the story. The messengers tell the women:

> *Remember what he told you while he was still in Galilee,*
> *that the Human One must be handed over to sinners, be*
> *crucified, and on the third day rise again.*
>
> (Luke 24:6-7)

Yes, the women were afraid and perplexed. But according to Luke, do you know what their real problem was? The women were forgetful. They and the other disciples should have remembered what Jesus had been telling them all along. All that they ever needed to know to make sense of this moment and to face it with courage had already been told to them. They just needed to remember what Jesus had been teaching them since the beginning.

Do you want to know how to accept resurrection in your life today? Do you want to know how to embrace the uncertainty of fear and grief?

According to Luke, it's through remembrance. Embracing the uncertainty and accepting the Resurrection lie in remembering that God has been working in you, whether you realize it or not, and has already given you everything you need to embrace new life.

Luke's message is inviting you to think back through some of the most significant moments of your life and see if you can remember...

- Do you remember what baptism means? That in your baptism God claimed you, welcomed you as God's own child, and was well pleased with you?
- Do you remember times in your life when you felt like there was something out there in the universe bigger than your own finite existence?
- Do you remember those moments when all seemed hopeless, when you were reaching out into the dark, and you could feel the tug of a guiding hand that would not let you give up?

God's grace has been at work your entire life, and at this moment, this very moment, the Easter story is giving you this key to new life: Remember who God is. Remember you are God's child. And remember what you already know about how you are to live.

Now, that really ought to be the end of the story right there. That ought to be it. Luke has already given us the big reveal. The Easter story, for all practical purposes, should be over.

Except Luke isn't done. For some reason, he has one more thing to say.

Because it is not until *now* that Luke chooses to reveal the women's names.

The other Gospels reveal the names at the beginning, but Luke waits until now, after they have already heard the news of the Resurrection and have gone to report it to the eleven disciples. Only then do we find out who the women were:

> *Mary Magdalene, Joanna, Mary the mother of James, and the other women with them.*
>
> (Luke 24:10)

In other words, among those women who first heard of Jesus' resurrection were Mary Magdalene, the prostitute and object of public scorn; and Joanna, the wife of an employee of Herod, one of the villains in this story.

These women had scandal in their past and baggage in their reputation. They were all carrying with them reasons why no one should believe a word they had to say.

That's exactly what happened when they told the disciples what they had seen. When they spoke to the eleven, we read, "Their words struck the apostles as nonsense, and they didn't believe the women" (Luke 24:11). The disciples didn't believe, and they thought the women were speaking nonsense.

Why? Not just because they were women in a patriarchal society. And not just because the news was hard to believe. It was also because the disciples could not let go of all the baggage these women carried from their past. They couldn't forget it.

Ultimately, Luke's Easter story is about competing memories. It is about making a choice between which set of memories you will choose to claim today. Will you choose to remember all the reasons why your life isn't worthy of God's love? All the shame and guilt from your past, all those ways in which you are too weak and undeserving of resurrection? If you do, then you will see this resurrection as nonsense, just like the disciples did.

Or will you choose to remember what God has been telling you all along? Will you choose the memories of God's love actively at work in your life? Will you choose to remember your baptism and remember that you are God's child? Will you choose to remember evidence throughout your life that in Christ, you have been given the power to face your future with clarity and not confusion, with fearlessness and not fright?

If you do, then on this day, your new life can start right here.

John: The Intimate Encounter (John 20:1-18)

If you read John's Gospel expecting to hear about the dramatic rising of Jesus from the tomb, you won't find it. You won't find any dazzling special effects—no thundering earthquake, no dazzling white angel that appears like lightning. You will find all that stuff in Matthew, but not in John.

Instead, John wants to build the suspense. He wants to keep a secret. He doesn't want to give away the ending until just the right moment. When the timing is right, when the moment is rich, when everything is in alignment, he will reveal his secret.

But not quite yet.

John decides to spin out something like a good detective novel. He lays out clue after clue for the characters to investigate. If John were alive today, you might half-expect to find him on the team of writers for *CSI* or *Law & Order*. He knows how to unpack a good mystery.

First to appear at the crime scene was Nancy Drew, played by Mary Magdalene. She discovered Exhibit A: the stone was rolled away (John 20:1). She returned with backups: Detective Columbo, played by Simon Peter; and The One Jesus Loved, John himself (20:2-3). John poked his head in to discover Exhibit B: burial linens lying unwrapped in the tomb (20:4-5). And Peter discovered the final clue when he looked inside: the head linen, separate from the others, rolled neatly into place (20:6-7).

Slowly, John peels back the layers of evidence, and just when you think he is ready to announce the great news to the world, he delays it even longer. Mary (and by implication Peter and John as well) comes to the conclusion that Jesus' body was stolen (20:13)!

There are many reasons to like this version of the Easter story. Rather than the dazzling, spectacularly dramatized events in some of the other Gospels, this one is driven more by dialogue, conversation, and relationships. There is a tender quality to it.

The biggest reason I like this version so much is the way that it accurately describes the human condition, particularly in the person of Mary.

She had just experienced the death of her teacher and friend. Upon arriving to do her duty and honor him, she discovers that the body had been stolen away. The discovery adds even more misery to her already tortured life, and there is a part of us that understands every bit of what she must have felt. Verse 11 of John 20 captures her state—and ours—very well: "Mary stood outside near the tomb, crying."

Two angels appear. In other Gospels, the angel or angels appear to announce the good news. "Do not be afraid," they say elsewhere. "He is not here," they say in other places. But here, in John, the focus is not on the news, but on the grief: "Woman, why are you crying?" (John 20:13).

And what's more, someone who looks like the gardener appears. He arrives to discover Mary weeping and asks her the same question: "Woman, why are you crying? Who are you looking for?" (John 20:15).

Then listen to Mary's response: "Sir, if you have carried him away, tell me where you have put him and I will get him" (John 20:15).

Here we are, fifteen verses into John's Easter story, and still not a word about the Resurrection. Still no revelation to the characters and to John's hearers about the reality of that first Easter morning.

And Mary, maybe just like you, is waiting.

You may have been waiting for God to puncture through your suffering with great drama and bravado. Maybe you have been searching for the kind of God we see in the other Easter stories, who breaks in like an earthquake, displays power by rolling away stones, and snaps us to attention with the voice of an angel.

And you're still waiting.

It was at that moment, when Mary was at the lowest point in her entire life, that John said, "It's time." Time to reveal the secret. Time to stop playing games, time to end the delay. The news that we all knew would come finally arrives, a full sixteen verses into the Gospel story.

The news comes not with the sound of trumpets, or earthquake, or angels. The news comes plainly, simply, and tenderly from the mouth of Jesus—the gardener himself.

He said her name.

"Mary!"

And when Mary heard her master utter her name, the fog lifted. Her ears were unstopped. Her eyes saw clearly. Jesus needed to say no more. "She turned and said to him in Aramaic, 'Rabbouni' (which means *Teacher*)" (John 20:16).

Listen very carefully. At this moment, this same God is whispering your name.

May you hear it with clarity. May you receive it with great joy. This same God who first uttered your name at the moment of your birth, who repeated your name when you were claimed at your baptism— this God calls out your name right now with the confidence of resurrection power.

You need no longer wait for your light to come. Your name is called. Your redeemer has come. Your risen Savior is here.

The idea of a dead person rising back to life may be hard to believe. It bucks our rational sensibilities and defies logic. But the impact of Jesus Christ's resurrection may be even harder to comprehend. For his resurrection changed the world. It declared God's power over sin and evil; it proclaimed and proved that death did not have the last word.

When we look around, we still see evidence of sin and suffering all around us, and it may hard to see any proof of the Resurrection at work today.

Each of the Gospel writers offers an answer to the uncertainty of God's resurrection power:

In Matthew, the Resurrection is found when we choose to live it, practice it, and follow God until we can fully believe it.

In Mark, the evidence for the Resurrection is found in the way God has worked in your past, before you even realized it, and is working in your future, to make you more like Jesus.

In Luke, resurrection is found in remembrance, choosing to believe in God's grace instead of the shame and guilt from your past.

And in John, resurrection is found in hearing God speak your name, and in realizing that God is always with you, despite all your uncertainties.

Reflection Questions

1. Of the four Gospel versions of the Easter story, which one speaks to you most profoundly right now? Why?
2. Was there a part of any of the four Gospel stories that surprised you in some way? What part was it, and how did it change your view of the Resurrection?
3. What questions do you still have about the resurrection of Jesus? How might you explore answers to those questions?
4. The Gospels seem less interested in explaining how the Resurrection happened, and more interested in who did the resurrecting and how humans are to be transformed because of it. How does that give you a deeper appreciation for what happened on that first Easter morning?
5. How will you embrace the certainty of the Resurrection?
6. How does confidence in the Resurrection enable you to embrace the uncertainty of life with faith?

Embracing the Uncertain

Each of the Easter stories in the Gospels calls for our response to the resurrection of Jesus. As you think about each version, what is the unique response that God is calling you to make in each Gospel? Write down those four ways that God is inviting you to experience resurrection, and review them every day for the next fifty days, between now and Pentecost Sunday. At Pentecost, give thanks for the way you are living out the Resurrection more than you were before.

Prayer

God, it is with amazement and profound gratitude that I claim your resurrection power. Thank you for not leaving me alone, and for raising me up to new life in Christ. Empower me to live in the peace, hope, and love that only you offer, and enable me to share the good news of Jesus with others. Amen.

NOTES

1   The text of the prayer can be found online at https://onbeing.org/blog
/thomas-mertons-prayer-that-anyone-can-pray/

2   Thomas Merton, *Thoughts in Solitude* (New York: Farrar, Straus, and
Giroux, 1999), 79.

3   Everett L. Worthington, Jr., "The New Science of Forgiveness,"
Greater Good Magazine, September 1, 2004, http://greatergood
.berkeley.edu/article/item/the_new_science_of_forgiveness. Accessed
August 7, 2017.

4   Joshua Lancette, "5 Ways Forgiveness Can Improve Your Health,
Backed by Science," http://joshualancette.com/forgiveness/. Accessed
August 7, 2017.

5   James A. Harnish, *Strength for the Broken Places* (Nashville: Abingdon,
2009), 94-95.

6   Desmond Tutu, "'I am sorry' – the three hardest words to say,"
The Guardian, March 22, 2014, https://www.theguardian.com
/lifeandstyle/2014/mar/22/archbishop-desmond-tutu-sorry-hard-to
-say. Accessed August 7, 2017.

7   Ibid.

8   Ibid.

9   C. Michael Hawn, "History of Hymns: 'His Eye Is on the Sparrow,'"
https://www.umcdiscipleship.org/resources/history-of-hymns-his-eye
-is-on-the-sparrow. Accessed August 7, 2017.

10   "His Eye Is on the Sparrow," Civilla D. Martin, 1905; *The Faith We Sing*
(Nashville: Abingdon Press, 2000), 2146. stanza 1.

11   Alison Gopnik, "When Children Beat Adults at Seeing the World,"
The Wall Street Journal, February 16, 2017, https://www.wsj.com/
articles/when-children-beat-adults-at-seeing-the-world-1487266807
?mod=djcm_fb3plus_12916. Accessed August 7, 2017.

12   Ibid.

13 "The Apostles' Creed, Traditional Version," in *The United Methodist Hymnal* (Nashville: The United Methodist Publishing House, 1989), 881.

14 Henri J. Nouwen, *Our Greatest Gift: A Meditation on Dying and Caring* (New York: HarperCollins, 2009), 19-20.

15 Anthony Bloom, *Beginning to Pray* (New York/Mahwah, NJ: Paulist Press, 1970), 41-42.

16 Ibid., 42.

17 Quoted in Lester Ruth, *Early Methodist Life and Spirituality* (Nashville: Kingswood, 2005), 122-123.

18 Ibid.